BODY against BODY

Edited by Elizabeth Zimmer and Susan Quasha

BODY against BODY

the dance and other collaborations of

Bill T. Jones & Arnie Zane

Station Hill Press

Published by Station Hill Press, Inc., Barrytown, New York 12507 with support
from the Howard Gilman Foundation, without whose financial assistance this
book would not have been possible.

Distributed by The Talman Company, 150 Fifth Avenue, New York, New York
10011.

The Publisher wishes to thank the photographers represented in this book for
permission to reproduce their works, which are copyrighted in the name ac-
companying each photograph. All reproduction rights reserved respectively to:
Perry Adleman, Tom Brazil, Barry Butterfield, Tom Caravaglia, Tseng Kwong
Chi, Dee Conway, Kenneth J. Cooper, Paula Court, James R. Dean, Johan
Elbers, Betty Freeman, Lois Greenfield, Chris Harris, Robin Holland, Jim Jen-
kins, Ifkovits Johannes, Susan Kuklin, Robert Mapplethorpe, Frank Ockenfels,
P. Quant, Peters Sayers, Niklaus Stauss, Nathaniel Tileston, Maya Wallach,
Bruce Wrighton, and Arnie Zane.

The Publisher gratefully acknowledges the following publications for permission
to reprint excerpts from articles indicated in the text and cited in the Bibliography: *City Arts, New York Newsday, The New York Times, The Village Voice,*
and *The Washington Post*; and Connie Kreemer's book *Further Steps: Fifteen
Choreographers on Modern Dance* (New York: Harper & Row, 1987).

Cover photo by Lois Greenfield.
Half-title photo by Paula Court (*Rotary Action*, 1984).
Frontispiece photo by Chris Harris (*Blauvelt Mountain*, 1980).
Designed by Susan Quasha.

Library of Congress Cataloging-in-Publication Data

Jones, Bill T.
  Body against body.

  Bibliography: p.
  1. Jones, Bill T. 2. Zane, Arnie, 1948-1988.
3. Choreographers—United States—Biography. I. Zane, Arnie, 1948-1988. II.
Zimmer, Elizabeth.   III. Title.
GV1785.A1J66   1988   729.8'2'0922   [B]   88-4930
ISBN 0-88268-064-1 (pbk.)

Manufactured in the United States of America.

Contents

Preface   7

Origins   9

    Bill T. Jones and Arnie Zane: Their childhood and early
    years together

Writings/Photographs: A Portfolio   22

    Poetry and prose of Bill T. Jones and visual imagery of
    Arnie Zane

Collaborations   52

    The dance works of Bill T. Jones/Arnie Zane & Co. and
    their various collaborators

Afterwords   119

Chronology of Premieres: 1971-1989   127

    Collaborations: Bill T. Jones/Arnie Zane & Co.

    Choreography by Bill T. Jones

    Choreography by Arnie Zane

Company Members   142

Selected Bibliography   143

Preface

Anyone with an eye on contemporary dance knows these two, knows that one is black and one white, one tall and the other short, one a talker and the other a maker of furiously original visual imagery. We know their seductiveness, their style, their daring. In just over ten years, Bill T. Jones and Arnie Zane left the hills of upstate New York and attained a critical and popular reputation of international magnitude.

This volume attempts to capture something about their lives, to record their work in modes other than dance, and to embody a very particular process: the emergence of art from collaboration. Accordingly, it is structured in three parts—an account of their origins, a selection of Bill's writing and Arnie's photography, and a montage of conversation, reportage and photojournalism which records their many and varied collaborative efforts. It calls on hours of personal interviews, dozens of transcripts, a huge file of reviews, and photographic archives stretching back more than fifteen years. The portrait photography of Zane, and compositions in several forms by Jones, illuminate the sensibility and the choreography of these artists.

These pages document the independent and collaborative work of two gifted individuals and reveal the personal resources, little known to metropolitan audiences, that undergird the art we know and equip these choreographers so well for their collaboration with others. Arnie Zane's portfolio of photographs, which he printed himself, have travelled with him across oceans and from a rural to an exurban home base. Bill T. Jones tours with a notebook; many of his journal entries, dance texts, and poems deal with the insights and dislocation of the traveler.

We first wish to acknowledge our great indebtedness to The Howard Gilman Foundation, without whose financial assistance this book would not have been possible. And to Pierre Apraxine of the Howard Gilman Foundation, we express our deepest gratitude for his enthusiastic support.

Many designers, directors, composers, artists, and other chore-ographers took the time to share their responses to working collaboratively with Jones and Zane. Numerous photographers have recorded these dancers and have generously allowed us to reproduce their work. To Paula Court and Tseng Kwong Chi, who graciously offered their time and work, we are deeply grateful. And to Lois Greenfield, Tom Caravaglia, Nathaniel Tileston, Chris Harris, and other photographers, our thanks for the enormous contribution to the record of the Jones/Zane oeuvre, and for allowing us to reprint their work. To Burt Supree, Deborah Jowitt, Alan M. Kriegsman and other journalists, our gratitude for providing clear articulation of their experience of the dances, and to Connie Kreemer, in her massive labor of interviewing the artists for her 1987 volume, *Further Steps*. Susan Quasha with infinite patience and great skill, assisted by George Quasha and Chris O'Brien, made huge piles of raw material into a book.

I have tried, calling on the words and images of Bill, Arnie, and scores of others, to conjure something like an invitation to their Valley Cottage home, an aisle seat in a downtown theater, a privileged position in the eaves of Soho lofts when collaborating artists are at work. I am assuming that those who read *Body Against Body* either cherish the dances already or will soon be inspired to get to know them.

Elizabeth Zimmer
New York City
March 1988

Monkey Run Road (1979)
Warren Street Performance
Loft
photo: Nathaniel Tileston

ORIGINS

Bill T. Jones, third grade

"I was always considered not a good-looking person. He was maybe going to be a preacher," he says of the boy he was, "and he was intelligent. He was not one of the pretty children. It wasn't until the past two years that I decided I didn't need to wear my glasses all the time."

—Bill T. Jones to Burt Supree
The Village Voice, 1981

Bill T. Jones was born on February 15, 1952 to Estella and Augustus, migrant farm workers in upstate Steuben County, New York.

Arnie Zane (1950)

"Zane is white, shorter, and more explicit, more forceful, harder-edged than Jones; he reminds me sometimes of those star-shaped weapons ninjas and other baddies throw in 007 movies."

—**Burt Supree**
The Village Voice, 1981

Arnie Zane is a first-generation American, born September 26, 1948.

The tenth of twelve children, Bill's siblings are Harris, Janie Mae, Roosevelt, Richard, Ivy Lee, Azel, Flo, Rhodessa, Johari, Stevenson and Gus Jr. They were among a handful of black families in the neighborhood. Bill excelled in high school theater and athletics. He knew he would be some kind of performer.

Estella and Augustus Jones (c. 1948)
photo: Arnie Zane

Flo, Bill T., Vilena, and Rhodessa Jones
photo: Arnie Zane

Judy, Arnie and Bobby Zane

Arnie is the second son of Orlando Zumpano, Italian Catholic immigrant from Brazil, and Edith Zacklin, Orthodox Jewish immigrant from Lithuania. They made up their last name.

Brother Robert was two years older, athletic, husky. He and his father were "real jock types," reflects Arnie, while his mother "had lots of spirit, and was interested in animals." Arnie and his mother had a large vegetable garden in Monsey, New York, not far from the Rockland County town where he and Bill T. Jones made their home.

Orlando and Edith Zane

"I come from a violent place," Bill told Burt Supree of *The Village Voice* in 1981. "I think one of the first things I ever heard was screaming. People moving around. 'Get out of the way. Be quiet.' Standing when I was very young next to a state-trooper who seemed to be seven-feet tall—just the monolithic form in gray cloth, a gun at his side and white skin, standing in a room of black faces. And this first awareness I ever had of a white person was an authority presence which changed the chemistry of the whole room. Even my mother and father began to behave differently. So these feelings exist in me. And when I make work, I try to reflect back all of those things, as purely as possible. And to put them in a larger context."

Everybody Works (1976)
solo performance
photo: Barry Butterfield

The Zanes moved to Maspeth, Queens, where Arnie, before catching the subway to Stuyvesant High School, worked in the family's luncheonette. His days were split between the latent racism of the Irish-Catholic neighborhood and the liberal atmosphere at Stuyvesant, where he attended classes "with a cross-section of highly intelligent young men—black, white, Hispanic, Asian. You did not have to feel self-conscious about your striving."

He learned North American Indian dances in the Boy Scouts, and social dancing at parties and Saturday record hops. "My body was raging to get out of Queens," he comments. "I was beginning to think I was the only person in the world like this. I developed a very sharp tongue for anyone who questioned my sexuality." He enrolled at the State University of New York at Binghamton in 1966, and studied theater and art history; not physically comfortable with himself, he thought he was too short to be a dancer.

Rumble in the Jungle (1983)

photo: Dee Conway

Jones always felt that he was a bisexual person. "In the migrant labor camps, there were drag queens. You never got in a fight with a 'faggot,' because you knew they had superhuman strength."

He enrolled at SUNY Binghamton to study theater and dance. In 1971, he met Arnie Zane. "I fell in love with a man. My sexuality was organized by the relationship."

Bill and Arnie (c. 1972)
photo: Barry Butterfield

Bill and Arnie (c. 1973)
photo: Arnie Zane

After graduation, with dreams of being a portrait photographer, Zane went to Europe on a charter flight: "the first stop was Amsterdam, and I just stayed." He got a job at a medical publishing company. "I was finding myself physically beautiful for the first time. People there were really trying to live the dream of the sixties, and it was really working."

He returned to Binghamton. In 1971, he met Bill T. Jones in the college pub. Thus began a sixteen year odyssey from a small college town to a large European capital, from New York State college dance departments to San Francisco, from Binghamton to Manhattan, from the small village of Valley Cottage to Manhattan and many European and American capitals, including the Kennedy Center in Washington, D.C.

Bill and Arnie: Valley Cottage Costumes
(1981)
photo: Paula Court

Cello in the Fields (1972)
photo: Arnie Zane

It is a bumpy ride, but always ends up back in the country, in a small house renovated to let in the sky. It is told in the poetry and prose of Bill T. Jones, the photography of Arnie Zane, the commentary of friends, collaborators, and critics.

Artists are often difficult to live with. Necessarily selfish, they frequently form relationships with helpmates willing to serve. Bill and Arnie are both strong characters, uncompromising in their vision. Can a marriage sustain two sovereigns? Can a dance company have two artistic directors? A few years ago I asked Arnie how things were going. "It's great," he said. "We're in social therapy now. If anything goes wrong, more than the relationship is at stake. We're a corporation."

The astonishing thing about their collaborative relationship is not that it has produced so much stimulating choreography, but that it has produced anything at all. The aesthetics of the two artists could not be more at odds. Bill T. Jones operates from the premise that his feelings are of value, that he wants to make room for them in his dancing. "Life is a vale of sorrow," he has said; "if I can get on stage and reveal my inner life, it would be valuable."

"If I were a brilliant technician," says Jones, "maybe I'd be showing people the potential of the human body. If I were an incredible poet, I'd want to put words together that move people and lift them up and transform them. If I'm an honest and concise enough performer, which I hope to be, I can present myself, my efforts, as an example of a world in which anything is possible. There are no holds barred in a world in which the imagination is striving to be free. In this era, that's an important thing to get across. We don't—most of us—really believe that we have beauty in us."

Arnie Zane is image-driven, a photographer first, using even the fluidity of contact improvisation as "an image from which you could make movement."

Bill's teachers, including Percival Borde and Pearl Primus, saw his talent and tried to send him to New York to "finish" his technique with Alvin Ailey. But the two men had other ideas.

Arnie took Bill to Amsterdam, and they both got jobs. Bill studied at the Cor Poleman School of Jazz Ballet. "I was interested in yoga, Eastern religions, spiritual pursuits." They were briefly devotees of Krishna Consciousness. They did the usual menu of drugs. "We were living at the edge, quite at odds with the world we were trying to exist in." Arnie was recording the images of people he found to be visually exciting. "At first I was interested in taking pictures of beautiful people, or beautiful pictures. As I got interested in dance, I got less interested in beautiful pictures. I started doing images of people who were falling apart—old people, people from mental institutions, people nude, to show the degeneracy of the body. Dance is one of the greatest words in the English language. It encompasses everything from being born to dying."

Marya
photo: Arnie Zane

The following is Burt Supree's 1981 account in *The Village Voice*: "Jones says, 'I used to prod Arnie to become more physical. He was a very visual person, he had quite a success with his photographs from the beginning.' Zane, with some measure of beginner's luck, got a show in Rochester of portraits he'd taken on a European trip with an inexpensive borrowed camera. He got a CAPS grant, bought himself a good camera. 'I started doing torsos of people of all ages, from bodies that were devastated to the very beautiful. I photographed the person from just beneath the eyes to the groin. This coincided with my developing as a dancer. I wanted the torso to bring the personality out. I wanted to be able to look at an anonymous person, like in a medical photograph, look at their torso and tell all about the persona.'"

Self-Portrait (c. 1978)
photo: Arnie Zane

Frank (1975)
photo: Arnie Zane

Pearl (1975)
photo: Arnie Zane

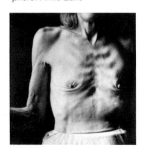

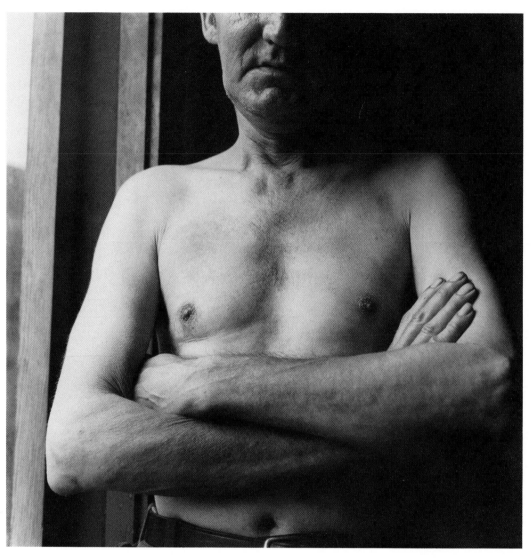

Walter (1975)
photo: Arnie Zane

Amsterdam (1971)

WRITINGS/PHOTOGRAPHS:
Bill T. Jones & Arnie Zane
A Portfolio

Binghamton (1974)
photos: Arnie Zane

South Hill

The cloth, my mantle, the wet stage of life.
Just out of some adolescent water, wet,
shivering, moving through reeds, grasses, thorns.
We've already passed the warm humidity of lakeshore
and now survey the sunset
rifling through hill's hair as mother's hand across
her small son's head.
For lack of things better to do while walking, not speaking,
we look at our hands—there are so many.
They dangle and pause about us, leading, following,
full of strength and exasperation.
Your hands are handsome in a blunt persistent way.
They've no love of book but enjoy each other greatly.
I like the way they clean each other like cats,
how they fit together like lovers, or like cloistered nuns.
We've reached hill top and below is a highway and waiting car.
How foolish to fight the chill with
nothing more than drenched clinging underwear
stuck in the crack of one's ass, lopsided
as our buttocks are alternately lopsided
in a race for the car.
It's much too late in the season for swimming.
Your grinning neck, a trickle of lakewater and
the sunlight ridicule regret,
disaster of heart or body, pain of death,
intrigue and failed ambition.
"Quick, start her up!"
"Turn off the fan till the engine warms."
"Who gives a damn?"
"Did you see that egret?"
"What a sunset."
"Let's go."

Getting Ready (1978)
Karen Calder, Jeanne Lee,
Bill T. Jones, Rhodessa Jones
photo: Arnie Zane

Valley Lilacs

Hello,

This is to tell you about the ugliest Lilac bouquet,
so ugly I could not bring it into the house!
No vase could enhance or alter this fact.
Here was a marvelously ugly bouquet.
My hill is riotous with lilacs.
On a park bench in Berlin
a victim of too much food and drink, not enough sleep,
I envisioned my hill burdened with lilacs I would
never see. My God! was I wrong.
Just look at these hussies clumped together full
of sweet stink there by the porch.
Over here by the garage, splayed open,
cheeky, voluptuous at the juncture of two trees,
Catching a bit of breeze and moving as
brown girls do beneath cheap jersey dresses.
And yet my ugly bunch smelled sweetest, most fragile.
I hold the virgin sacrifice of lilacs.

There is a small red shack with what is left of a red roof.
I call it the garage though it's full of miscellany
I've nowhere else to tuck away in this world.
It stands sentinel on my hill, painted front to the road.
At one corner there is an ancient lilac bush.
I'm tempted to call it a community of lilacs, of old lilacs
Outlandish in an arrested configuration of collapse.
For five years I've promised to cut them back
but each spring at this time I am hypnotized by
an outrageous display of blossoms cantilevered,
offered to the eternal spaces so serenely generous,
optimistically profiled as the feather on a drunken woman's hat
or a half opened fan falling from her hand.
well to be sure I did decide to cut her or them back
Each of these twisted rivers of cellulose and bark seemed
to forgive me as they fell. I was the commandant
sawing at a crowd, deciding who should live or die.
Some of them, though dried out and dead
were striving to produce blossoms—sickly, stunted,
half-formed, but blossoms.

On the Hill in Johnson City (1972)
photos: Arnie Zane

They offered these to me like old men who hand
over their grandchildren to soldiers and are
led away to the slaughter.
As the surgeon and executioner I bundled these offerings
sniffed each one slowly
then gave them the dignity of rot
on the trash heap further down my hill.
As I write this my hands smell of cut grass, gasoline,
and fragrant murder.

Amsterdam (1971)
photo: Arnie Zane

Binghamton (1974)
photos: Arnie Zane

Evening to the Outhouse

I can remember a summer evening when dark was a huge awe descending on me, a six-year-old boy. I was with my mama as we left the stone house and were heading for the shadows of the toilets, hurrying as if to outrun the complete darkness and knowing it would overtake us. Mama, I remember so well, she was a big lush woman-thing, her face floating beneath the reddest of work bandanas. This bandana, the dusty dress, and overalls gave testimony to a workday's end. Night's rituals began and of course this short journey was first.

I was jiggling and jumping down the path and of course she didn't understand it was simple ecstasy to be alone with her, and awash in her complete attention; for we seemed to have left the earth and were instead cruising through some oily liquid. The sky became a fantastic ocean reflecting streaks of sunset giving way to stars that appeared like tiny sea animals rising to the surface, each offering a phosphorescent belly. This celebration didn't concern itself with busy earthflames cooking food or even the short-lived sparks snapping and cracking with insane challenges. Suddenly one of those stars flashed and I grabbed it only to find it had wings with a glowing tail. Even though we'd been speaking of growing up I was momentarily lost in that firefly until Mama reclaimed my attention with the melody of her voice echoing from within the old wood. Inside there was a pause, the toilet paper whispered, and I asked how long must it be before I'm a teenager; she rebounded with a casual "soon enough." Even that seemed too long, so I tried to object but the earth let go a sigh that dissolved my objection like smoke, so I held my breath and there was silence cut across as the tiny door creaked open emitting the great outline of one black woman who felt the nightscene with her eyes, then reached for me, drew me close and headed back to the light.

**Rhodessa and Darkie at
Tomato, San Francisco**
(1974)
photo: Arnie Zane

Untitled

Duchampian sequitur!
The fight is on.
Figuration as parallel to characterization.
"Alas, poor Yorick! I knew him well, Horatio!"
The Dance is "the retarded child of incestuous parents."
The Dance is "the Sleeping Beauty."
The Dance is dead and risen.
The american lady "sees america dancing."
The Dance is pastime of Cultural terrorist.
"What if we kidnapped Merce Cunningham?"
The Dance is aerobics for amputees.
The Dance is a Ballet Lobotomy
          is a study in ritualized seduction.
Their Dictum: A pursuit of the impeccable gesture.
Their Modus: The domestication of bodily violence.
Their Creed: Our insides are now outside!
the future?
    We plan to rechoreograph the original
assault on Omaha Beach in Normandy.
But first please repeat after us
Yea though I (walk,spin,slide and run) through
the Valley of Death I shall fear no evil for
thou Art with me "Amen!"

Pacifica, San Francisco
(1974)
photo: Arnie Zane

Monologue I
August 25, 1982

There were miles and miles of highway stretching away at that time. The people were all moving on that highway, going north or south, to that job or this. Big Mama, my mother's mother, said she would "grab herself a handful of greyhound and be up north in a minute." I travel the skies more than highways now. But yes, there are cars, trains, buses and airplanes. The people all stand so peculiarly at airports. Bigheaded babies, mothers looking for fathers flying in from Tokyo; chic straight-backed dancers and round black ladies wrapped like Christmas from Sierra Leone. The people all read newspapers. In the papers they mention my dancing or what I or where I plan to dance. They sometimes quote my words. It's hard to read one's words in the newspaper. The people think about their houses, children, wives and presidents. I think about that section in the dance wherein he takes me on his back and I don't quite come off the ground. I often make dances as if they were the movements one might make as the sidewalk exploded. We are reflected in the plate glass. There are old women on lawn chairs. They are watching children dancing. It's a dance about a river. It could be Isadora Duncan and her kids doing the Blue Danube Waltz. She is now dancing with the kids on Route 17 that winds past the Hudson, through the Catskills, through Binghamton, Corning, and Elmira heading west. The roads are still moving north or south or somewhere. People are travelling the roads and listening to music. They are reaching into the back seat to get a beer, quiet the kids or find a camera. They are chewing toast in roadside luncheonettes or sipping coke from the can on the New York State Thruway. People have to stand up sometimes and stretch. I'm stretching like Isadora's long-legged America stretches from coast to coast, from waking to dreaming. People are not dreaming. I'm not dreaming either. We are all awake. We sometimes talk intelligently when we are awake. We discuss the force/fulcrum principle in society and art and speak softly and sometimes we are screaming. Some people are large and stupid. Some people have thick skulls and skin. If the skull is like an egg then the skin must be thick. My father used to sit for hours watching television. He would sit and shake his foot. My mother would say "Gus, what you looking at on TV?" He would say, "I ain't looking at it, I'm looking through it." My father and all the people watch TV. We've all looked at it. I can't always look through it, however. I

Found Image, Holland
(c.1972)
photo: Arnie Zane

Train, Nevada (1977)
photo: Arnie Zane

Found Image (c. 1975)
photo: Arnie Zane

get caught in it sometimes. I love to watch dancing anywhere, on TV, whatever. I love to watch people learning to dance. I love to watch them in ballet class. I wonder what they are thinking, where they will go or where they have been. Who they have said good-bye to? Where will they lie down, or fall down, or sit down to die? I love to watch people, some of whom are doctors or lawyers or sick or rich or communists or homosexuals. Some are writers or dancers or TV makers, mothers or bus drivers. People love to watch people too, I think. Do they love to watch people dancing? Do they care how an arm is raised, or how a back is scooped or how someone's weight is passed into the floor?

At the Crux of (1976)
photo: Arnie Zane

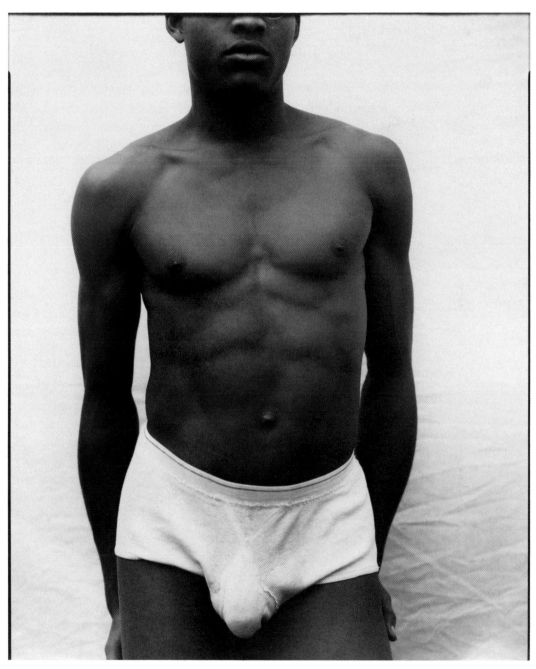

Bill (1974)
photo: Arnie Zane

Untitled

At this time ideas are actions or they are nothing at all.

Well, at this time we took a bow, sweat covering everybody, cheeks and hands. We ran off like players when the game is over. In our case however no one was quite sure whether they had won or not. Nonetheless there were kisses all around and meaningful embraces and farewells in the dressing room and at the cast party later.

At this time events seem to streak by and I am sitting alone in a deserted cafeteria watching an insane man limp through a soliloquy of speech and song. He reminds me of a searing hot day on Canal Street when another mad performer stopped traffic wearing a cardboard box as a headdress, a regal robe of rags, and shoes that covered only the tops of his feet. He oozed across the blistering crosswalk like King Lear. There was something in what he said and how he moved that makes me remember him burning. At this time, performing for a congregation of strangers, I beg him to come into my body. Percy Borde used to tell us of the supplicants in Haiti who would dance for hours until the spirit of Dhambala shot through their spines, causing them to undulate in spasm like a cobra about to strike. At this time I am turning and others are moving 'round me, sometimes real and sometimes imagined. I am turning in my head, my feet and backside all simultaneously. There are others moving past like Einstein's trains hurtling through a void that is not as infinite as one might think. It's the idea of a void. I'm the idea of turning or walking. IDEAS ARE REAL! IDEAS ARE REAL? At this time I remember walking into a museum years ago looking for a particular sculpture exhibit. I saw the title on the wall but couldn't find the piece. I stumbled over six wooden pegs like toadstools pushing up out of the carpet and suddenly the idea was revealed. I didn't know if I like it or not but at least I could recognize it. At this time, sweat, cracked feet, age and audience are more real than ideas. Standing in a spot of light, grabbing his or her hand, going down under that one's weight, are quite real. At this time memories can be more real than sensations. I took a walk with my mother at age five. She went into the wooden outhouse as I played outside. It was dusk in summer. I asked her how long does it take to become grown. She said I would find out soon enough. I took a walk with a ten-year old from the midwest in New York. I wasn't sure if I should hold her hand or put an arm around her shoulder so instead we walked side by side with arms free and swinging. She made remarks about the height of all the buildings, the strangeness of the people and how I walked "funny." I took a walk through the British Museum and came before three marble fragments of women dancing that symbolized the breeze. Without thinking my arms raised and I balanced my toes. The color of the museum guard's hat and shoes brought my heels to the ground.

At this point I project into the future. I now weigh 60 lbs more. I move in a circle of former "this and thats," I wear expensive suits when I go to performances of my friends' children making a debut here, or showing there. I have fewer ideas and more patience. I say goodbye easier. I've seen hundreds of airports, train stations and taxi cabs. The entire world is several hours wide. My image and the image of others twenty, thirty, forty years ago are no more than the press of a button away. At this point ideas are actions or they are nothing at all.

Port Royal Sound (1973)
Bill T. Jones in a play by
Azel Jones
photo: Arnie Zane

Union Square
April 1985

Almost impossible
the gentle precision of a construction crane
twenty stories high.
This vertical vector, mute
defines what is to become no longer empty—
new luxury housing, a sad intrusion
on the perfect air.
Another upended crate of glass and steel.

Sometimes we are small, nervous
like children chastised,
or the wives of dead rebels
maybe mothers amid the rubble
when all digging stops
and there ceases to be quiet tapping
underground.

We become pensive,
unsettled, disorganized by such
vertical organization.
you say we are not thoughtful, but angry.
Poor anger—tearing at a pillow,
another scream in the nursery.
Why argue?
Yes, we are angry.
We have so little understanding
of the world's devious meshings,
history's force and fulcrum,
the metallic, sometimes creaking
language of lies, poorly conceded truths,
the verticality of power
  (the round house)
its truncheon pace
    (the slow punch)
unhurried
with such grace
so high

above.

Doing the One Step (1974)
photo: Arnie Zane

Untitled

ignoble yet most reliable
my view of time
the lady politician comments
"They say time heals."
I say
"It just passes."
In her case a beloved father was killed
In ours I have the slow procession
of hours that will take you away from me.
You've not left yet. Don't go!
Make death a weak incompetent thief,
who comes into our house, stumbles
in the dark and leaves with nothing,
not your smile,
not your feel
your eyes
your smell
nothing
the bastard dolt gets nothing.

I see the city from above.
Just as the red west flares
and the ocean shore east becomes smoke
What a great moment to end with!
An earthly masterpiece
distant below, the elements
fissioning with bliss
into sleep

there is the slow inevitable descent
there is leaving the thing
the air ship, the metal fish
then there is asphalt
chrome and carpet
there is a wait
a fat man on the telephone
a girl snaps by in high heels
an old black gentleman whistles
a revolving door partly obscured by a sign
spits and splices humanity into

Bill and Bowler Hat (1978)
photos: Arnie Zane

Pearl (1975)
photo: Arnie Zane

headless hips and legs.
The wait. This point of view
the door, the distance to
parked and moving automobiles.

You come
breathing full of concern,
tired perhaps,
a mission of purpose,
of agony.

You bring your church
with its dogma of love,
its chorus of salutation.
these are days, weeks,
months full of touching
of goodbyes and sweet spit
You come.

First Position (1975)
photo: Arnie Zane

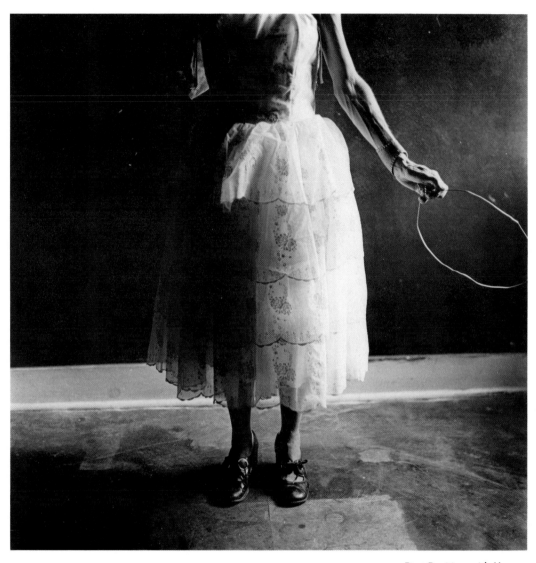

First Position with Hoop
(1975)
photos: Arnie Zane

Untitled

A few words about
leaving would seem
like nothing
if I were
gone.

                    I'm gone

already, shaking hands
with those who
brought me
and avoiding the eyes
of those who never
saw where I was headed.

                     I'm here

like standing playfully

forever

exalted at being

able to
really just stand playfully

forever

exalted at being.

Olympia's New Shoes
(c.1976)
photos: Arnie Zane

April 12, 1981

Daddy died April 1 at 1:00 am in San Francisco. He was born in Georgia. They are all there in the chapel. The others, "the dream persons," are in the background like the chorus moving in hushed unison as he lies, a waxed effigy in a maroon sports jacket and tie. His forehead is immense and cold as polyurethane. The structure of his head and face is echoed and silhouetted in all of us.

Rhodessa was present at Mt. Zion the night he died. I was listening on the phone when the doctor brought the news. She tells me that after the initial wailing and then a dumbstruck silence at the sight of his uninhabited body, all the women clustered around, stroking and touching him, still pliant and warm. She used her greedy loving fingers to decode the bones of his cheeks, forehead and chin, desperate to read the message that was certainly left there. She read something. As I sat with her a week later, her eyes shared as much as they could spare. We are wed through these faces, this shared code embedded in bone.

**Mama and The Vision of
Death** Port Royal Sound
photo: Arnie Zane

Untitled
1983

He learns by example.
A more porous intelligence you could not imagine.
It's an experimental (read artificial) intelligence.
At once mawkish and childlike, yet unable
to decipher motivation.
purely reactive?
Purely reactive intelligence though not entirely
passive.
How's that?
He sees the animal in its cage and responds
through imitation to its captivity.
What if he saw the animal rip apart
prey?
Oh! I see.
No I'm afraid you don't. You see he is beyond
morality and intellect, he is to be used.
He is to be flung at a target, to be mounted, to be dispatched,
reined in and releasing?
I'm sorry but we've run out of time. This interview is
to be ended.

First Portrait (c. 1973)
drawing
photo: Arnie Zane

First Portrait (1973)
photo: Arnie Zane

COLLABORATIONS

Rotary Action (1984)
background painting,
Tongue to the Heart, by
Robert Longo; Metro Pictures
Gallery, New York City
photo: Paula Court

Studio Portrait (1986)
photo: Robert Mapplethorpe

○

Bill Katz

Bill Katz
photo: Betty Freeman

"I was told the working title of this book was *Conflict and Collaboration*. How apt! Just the gritty edge of reality for these two people who have worked together so intimately for seventeen years. Immediately it conjured up recollections of a chair flying through rehearsal studio air, heated moral arguments at three star tables, solo appearances when duets had been announced—in short, the emotional content of an existence without a gap between life and art. The title has changed, but the word conflict—'a dashing together, as of waves'—stays vividly in mind.

"There are at least as many ways of collaborating as there are people working together, and over nearly two decades, I've been part of many collaborations. None have had the dynamic that Bill T. and Arnie occasion. Partly, it occurs because there are *two of them. They always have two* ideas, *two* ways of seeing, *two* ways of doing, at *once*. Yet, somehow, when work begins to flow, they pass ideas, movement and support seamlessly from one to the other so that the *and* in Bill T. Jones *and* Arnie Zane becomes the fulcrum.

"As responsive as they are to each other, so are they responsive to the work of others. Perhaps because of their own relationship, they are used to the sovereignty of the creator and so are able to truly include composers and artists in lively and intimate collaboration, with all the upfront, direct opinion they offer each other. Obviously they have decided that social glosses are not part of their character. Much more do they enjoy digging in and getting to the heart of the matter. They understand and relish the intricacies of social intercourse, the social contract and the social code— but they restructure and explore them as freely as they do the forms of classical and modern dance.

"Concerned both with a new vocabulary for dance and an urge to communicate, Bill T. Jones/Arnie Zane & Company (again the emblematic ampersand) have created dances both confrontational and tender, each as real as if it were a whole landscape and climate, untranslated, untranslatable, and unique."

—B. K.

●

Collaborating with each other and with others—Bill with dancers like Sheryl Sutton and Senta Driver and Arnie with Johanna Boyce—meant that each of them was constantly modifying the strong vision with which he had begun.

"I was compelled," Bill told Burt Supree in 1981, "to get Arnie more involved physically. I encouraged him to do yoga . . . . "

"It was terrible," Arnie interrupts, "I had tears in my eyes. Bill was trying to get me to do the plow. Three mornings in a row I was crying. The pain—from trying to put my toes to the floor behind my head."

"I don't know why I pushed him so," says Jones. "But sure enough, once he got a taste of it, he was quite precocious." "The best thing for me," says Zane, "was that, from the outset, people encouraged me to choreograph. It was lucky, because I wasn't about to put everything on hold while I took ten years to make my dancer's body."

Meanwhile, Bill was making work that was very personal. Says Arnie, "I was next to, and being compared with, someone I thought was one of the greatest modern dancers of my era, and I was not a highly trained dancer. I didn't want to share my personal life with an audience, and yet I wanted to work with this person. He was drawing my life into the performance arena. This was very frightening. People were incredibly attracted by this personal story. It was frightening to me to be developing as a sexual being, involved in an intimate relationship, and to be sharing it live, and on top of that having it criticized. I didn't really want to give as much. Bill really threw himself into the foray and gave. I wanted to walk away from it, if I could. Working with Bill was both extremely exhilarating and better than the best of sex— but the reality of touring was that we performed night after night, took train ride after train ride. That story had been told. We needed to develop, to learn how to make ensemble dancing."

○

Johanna Boyce

Arnie and I decided to work together because we have very similar physiques, short and stocky, and because we shared similar notions about postmodern choreography. Arnie had a history of collaboration. It was my first time working with another choreographer. It felt to me as if his incredible determination and optimism kept us industrious, while I nursed my anxieties about the work and the collaborative process. We both wanted our work to be visceral and physical, but we were particularly intent on conveying ideas about social and psychological concerns.

The movements of the German Expressionists intrigued us and, like them, we focused on physicality and form. With that as our movement theme we explored their emphasis on bodily and spiritual perfection, which initially pre-existed and then coincided with national socialism and ideas of Aryan supremacy. We wondered how something so healthy had co-existed with the atrocities of the Holocaust. We brought this question to bear through dialogue, movement and imagery. The title, *Garden*, suggested decomposition and rebirth; the burying and shoveling under of millions of Holocaust victims, and the hope that by not forgetting, it would be less likely to recur.

One evening while we were performing, someone went into our dressing room and stole a precious ring and watch of Arnie's. I remember his despair, and our shared feelings of helplessness and anger. We continued to perform and what I remember most about working with Arnie was his driving energy, his vibrant personality, and his love for, and belief in, the good life.

—J. B.

●

Johana Boyce and daughter Charlotte
photo: Robin Holland

**boyce
zāne**

IN
GARDEN

danspace - St. Mark's Church
2nd Ave. & 10th st.

Dec. 11,12,13,17,18,19   8 pm
Dec. 12,19   10 pm
reservations   674-8112

Garden Poster

Bill conducting children's dance workshop (c. 1977 – 78)

They returned to upstate New York, where they found a community including a handicapped neighbor with a swimming pool. "Bill and I have always had the blessing of being taken in. We're attracted to whatever pushes the boundaries. We had a very large garden, a little family, friends," says Arnie. One day Bill brought home a flyer about contact improvisation. Lois Welk, a dancer/ choreographer, taught a workshop, in which Bill and Arnie enrolled.

Lois Welk

○

"1973, Brockport, New York: I met Bill T. Jones (then William Jones) and Arnie Zane (then A.M. Zane, photographer). I was temporarily back on the East Coast, having left San Francisco to teach a contact improvisation workshop at SUNY Brockport. My path intersected Bill's at Hartwell Studio. He was coming in to use the space as I was finishing. I gave him the workshop flyer, which he carried home to the then non-dancing Arnie Zane.

"The workshop was scheduled to meet daily for 3-4 hours and although a fair-sized group showed up on the first day, the ranks dwindled quickly until no one was left except Bill, Arnie and me dancing for hours in an immense gym-converted-to-studio. We improvised our way toward a bonding that has lasted to this day.

The chemistry was exciting. Signals were easily sent and received between us. We hoped to rendezvous in San Francisco.

"1974, San Francisco, California: We went to work making dances immediately. A performance was created, rehearsed and ready to go in a matter of weeks. We performed our first concert as co-directors of the American Dance Asylum. Arnie's *Self-Portrait* and Bill's *A Christmas Story* were on the program.

"Shortly after that production we reversed our decision to locate in San Francisco. I had an intuition that we should all go to N.Y. State to be close to New York City. I missed the stimulation of more mature dance artists. I remember expressing this notion to Arnie, and then the three of us going for a walk to confer. The decision was the hardest for Bill who has family in San Francisco. By the end of the walk we had made our decision. Arnie knew of a large building we could probably rent inexpensively in downtown Binghamton. Our primary concern was access to space. We wanted to be within driving distance of Manhattan and in a community that might provide an audience. We were back in Upstate New York within the next two weeks. Jill Becker joined us there, and during our first year in Binghamton she was the fourth founding member of the American Dance Asylum.

Lois Welk
photo: P. Quant

"1974-9, Binghamton, New York: We worked and lived together. We were energized, ambitious, optimistic and naive. Each of us directed and choreographed our own productions, and were influenced by each others' aesthetics, ideas and kinetic language. A great deal of time was spent in the creation phase of the art. Many dances were only performed three or four times. As soon as one production closed, a new ADA poster was on the street announcing the next performance. There were from 8 to 12 dances (many evening-length productions) premiered annually.

"We each had a major impact on the shape of the work. Bill supplied a more classical dance sensibility, an intuitive understanding of the dramatic gesture, powerful athleticism and an interest in text/poetry. Arnie's keen visual sense impacted the art and the business of the American Dance Asylum. His kinetic language was percussive, charged, primal. His choreography reflected the severity of his photography.

"Empowered by our naivete and optimism we took countless risks together—financial, artistic and personal. The process of creating a dance was a dance."

—L. W.

●

**Everybody Works/All
Beasts Count** (1976)
performance with neighborhood children, Binghamton
photo: Barry Butterfield

Influenced by the spectacle-rejecting manifesto of Yvonne
Rainer, they played structuralist improvisational games as taught
by Richard Bull and Daniel Nagrin. They absorbed the writings
of Simone Forti and the work of several filmmakers, and were
inspired by the Judson Dance Theater and the Grand Union, incu-
bators for the personalities who are now the mainstream of contemporary dance: Steve Paxton, Lucinda Childs, David Gordon,
Trisha Brown, Douglas Dunn, Barbara Dilley, Yvonne Rainer, and
others.

In Brockport in 1975, they taught *Rhada, a real dance* to a large group of students. One reported that it was "an endurance dance; we jumped and we spun for hours. By the end of the dance, everybody was on another planet." They remained expressive and expressionistic through a period of minimalism. "We listened to jazz music a lot," Jones said, "and thought a lot about the improvisational relationships in a jazz quartet. It was expected that the end result was about saying something. We were interested, very much as we are now, in visual arts, music, all of the disciplines. We were greatly impressed by a wild filmmaker, Jack Smith, and by structuralist filmmakers like Ernie Gehr, Michael Snow, Tony Conrad. We were very distrustful of New York, and of anything slick."

Lois Welk says of this time, "We worked together in a subliminal way, making our own separate dances, relating to each other every single day. Every morning we did a class together. Bill and I rotated teaching; we did headstands, yoga, running, running backwards, contact warm-ups, improvisational structures. In these morning sessions, we processed each other's ideas. Then we rehearsed, then broke for lunch. We offered evening classes for the public at supper time."

Bill worked in a laundry and Arnie as a go-go dancer in a bar in a nearby town. They became producers, bringing experimental artists to mid-state New York. They performed in Lois Welk's structured improvisations, where movement was free but phrasing carefully measured. Finally they had to make a choice between being administrators of an experimental center and giving full attention to their own art. They sold the building, and Bill and Arnie began making the standard introductory forays into the New York City dance community. Bill had work shown at a Clark Center New Choreographers Series in 1976, and the following year *With Durga* was chosen for the Dance Theater Workshop's Choreographers Showcase.

In the fall of 1979, the two men moved down to Valley Cottage, an hour by car from midtown Manhattan. They were working on the trilogy that put them firmly on the international dance map: *Monkey Run Road* (1979), *Blauvelt Mountain* (1980), and *Valley Cottage* (1981).

Deborah Jowitt offered the following thoughts in *The Village Voice* (October 3, 1980): "The theater becomes an urban clearing in which some rite inexplicably vital to us all is taking place. We do not demand to understand the 'meaning' of what they're doing at every second or strain to hear a *sotto voce* conversation the way we might in a large proscenium theater; we do not sigh over repetition or wonder if carrying bricks is dancing. We do delight in noticing that we can never see the 'same' movement twice, that it is always changing either because of context or because of humaneness. And we see the performers at close range—close to eyes, minds, hearts."

Bill T. Jones said, in conversation with Connie Kreemer for her book *Further Steps*: "A landmark duet we made was *Blauvelt Mountain*, which was the centerpiece of a trilogy in 1979. Blauvelt combined structuralism with personal introspective poetry, some social issues, but not as much as the world brought to it. It was an extremely rigorous piece in two sections. The set was a simple brick wall about 6 feet at its highest point. All the material could have been performed in about 15 minutes, but instead it was accumulated movement. The sequence was maybe 40 movements long, but the first 10 would be shown, then the first 10 plus 20, and so on, moving around in the space. It had some speaking in it, *sotto voce*, speaking in very low voices, almost word association games. And yet, the structure was unraveling all the time so it could be enjoyed on that level. The dance brought many disparate elements between two people together, like an urban clearinghouse: one who is short and white and one who is tall and black. When we did it in Berlin, we were awarded the German Critics Award.

Blauvelt Mountain Act I:
"A Fiction" (1980) Bill T.
Jones and Arnie Zane,
rehearsal photograph with
costumes never used in performance.
photo: Lois Greenfield

"One thing I've learned, is that the world brings a great deal of baggage to each performance. We didn't bring as much to *Blauvelt Mountain* as the world did. The dance had been made a year before we ever came to Berlin, even thought about going there, and suddenly I woke up one morning and we were going to premiere the piece in Berlin.

"I said to Arnie, 'I don't believe we're going to do this here.' Because during the second act of *Blauvelt*, a cinder block wall is deconstructed by Arnie upstage and then reconstructed through the center of the space. And I said, 'I don't believe we're going to build a wall in this performance space here in Berlin.' Well, the Germans went crazy over it. They loved it. They read all sorts of things into it. They thought we were making statements about their society, about blacks and whites in America—we were not. We were making, for us, an abstract dance. It did have some word association in it, but that wasn't even as important as the way we went at it, repeated and sweated right there in front of them so they heard us breathing."

Blauvelt Mountain Act II:
"The Interview" (1980)
Washington Hall
Performance Gallery,
Seattle
photo: Jim Jenkins

Blauvelt Mountain (1980)
rehearsal photograph
photos: Lois Greenfield

Blauvelt Mountain Act I:
"A Fiction" (1980) Riverside
Studios, London
photos: Chris Harris

Valley Cottage I
Dancetext by Bill T. Jones

B It's in my muscles, it's in my genes.

A What is?

B A certain degree of tension.

A I try not to be self-conscious.

B Uh huh, and my reply is

A What?

B Uh huh.

A That's it. That's not a reply, it's not enough. Connect your reply to your muscles and your genes.

B Is that a play on words?

A Are you asking me? Answer me.

B Is it biology or a television commercial? Do you know what I mean?

A No.

B Jeans.

A Jeans! Very funny—

B It's Saturday. I didn't mean for it to be funny. I was really asking the question. It upset me to be sitting on the street there on Saturday—fur coats, blue jeans . . . .

A Foreign money, oil . . . .

B If I were wealthy I'd be a recluse. And I wouldn't talk to anybody I know now.

A I'd talk to about five to ten people I know now . . . . There's Ann . . . .

B How did you decide on that number?

A I thought right away of the people I dance with and left out most everybody else . . . . I have this dream of wearing long white clothes and I weigh about 175 lbs.

B Are you dead?

A No—my hair is real long—and I don't go to see dance and my dancing is just the daily process. You?

B I'd like to buy pictures and listen to music and have all my teeth when I die.

A You probably will . . . .

B I'd have to start running again, if I weren't dancing, to salvage my cardiovascular . . . .

A To hell with that.

B Huh.

A Just eat moderately, stretch . . . I think positively. That's it! That's the answer.

B You mean that's the formula . . . I like to eat.

A So do I . . . I like to eat, I like sex, like my dogs . . . I like

B Long black cars.

A What made you say that?

B Because I want to have a long black car.

A Well I'll be practical . . .

B Do you believe in sin?

A In a way.

B You either do or you don't.

A Well, it's not right to hurt anyone .

B But is it wrong? My brother used to sit on me and he'd say might has right.

II

B Isn't the beach beautiful? I thought we'd never get here. Let's go down to the water.

A It's kind of cold.

B Oh really? I thought it was very warm. It must be your circulation.

A Remember Gretchen's drawings?

B No. What made you think of that?

A I looked over at them.

B When?

A Just now.

B But it's not now, Arnold . . . . That's a long time ago.

A They're right there . . . . They're on the wall.

B Never mind that, let's go down to the water . . . .

A But we were just in the water . . . .

B You thought you were in the water, I thought you were in the air . . . . We've got to walk the distance from here to the water.

A She put her glasses on and arranged the photos on the wall.

B It's funny how people were making stuff then.

A She makes me think about my photos and all of the bodies I wanted to show. Jackie said they were too harsh; she couldn't look at them for too long. What was that guy's name—the French photographer? You know . . .

B Lumiere? No! that was film . . . no, Brassai . . . no . . . the little kid . . . that's right, you know, he became so mediocre when he grew up . . . . What was his name? Lartigue or Lartrique?

A Doesn't matter, we know who we mean—I never saw her like this, serious—she's beautiful, serious and inspirational—very French . . . .

Valley Cottage (1981) Bill T. Jones and Arnie Zane at The Kitchen, New York City
photo: Paula Court

B What did you say? You're confusing me, or were confusing me.

A It was like Matisse the way she kept taking those little photos and began putting them all up and the matte knife kept cutting. Can I borrow your sunglasses?

B You know they're prescription—I can't see a thing without them.

A Remember that award?

B Which one?

A The one that came by telegram. What about it?

B You brought it up . . . . What about your photographs?

A I love them like someone loves their family. She made me think about them.

B She makes you think about them? You should put some lotion on your shoulders.

A They're all so intense.

B Huh?

A You know . . . young artists constantly arranging, cutting—

B They're scared . . . .

A Are you?

B Let's go swimming . . . .

(For *Rotary Action*)

A   Make a speech.

B   Make a statement.

A   OK, it's my turn to begin.

B   Let me introduce you.

A   Waiting . . . .

B   Let's see. To hell with effect . . . . Look at that action? Got it?

A   Look at that.

B   Look at that.

A   I've got an idea.

B   What is it?

A   It's a play in my mind. A man takes a step, slips on an icy pavement, and lands on his ass. He's travelled 90 degrees.

B   You mean he's travelled . . . .

A+B   180 degrees.

A   OK. It's summer. There are two people, a body of water, and a band. You know, I don't understand "to hell with effect, look at that action."

B   It's a statement of purpose. It's simply the doing of it, like two arms going round and round.

A   The people are golden.

B   Golden?

A   They have brass smiles on their faces and the sounds from the band are flying above them.

B   You know, you're taking a lot of liberties.

A   What do you mean?

B   You're creating a fantasy for us. It's yours, not mine. My job is to join in and help you create your fantasy.

A   What's that?

B   What's a brass smile?

A   It's when a figure doesn't move but its mouth opens and holds a fixed position.

B   You mean like a dog that's gonna bite somebody.

A   What?

B   You know, a feral smile.

A   I'm not familiar with that word.

B   It's not really a smile, it's a grimace.

A   The band keeps playing and the notes move farther and farther from the people.

B   This is all very difficult to say.

A   It's only your memory.

Rotary Action (1983)
Riverside Studios, London
photo: Chris Harris

B   It's not just memory. It's connecting to words.
A   Connections to sounds, sound next to other sounds.
B   So you say . . . .
A   One more play, OK? What's this one gonna be about?
B   This one's gonna be about separation.
A   What do you mean separation?
B   I mean the fear of separation. Are you ready?

While on an Affiliate Artist's tour of educational environments in 1979, Bill told an interviewer at the Kent School in Connecticut that "to this point my work has originated almost exclusively in personal experiences. Now I am trying to take a direction more towards structuralism, or formalism, to take off my emotional garb and try to create a work coming purely from my concerns with space, with time, with movement—not so much with exorcising unwanted feelings or trying to tear the scabs off, or trying to heal through performing."

Break KTCA-TV (1983)
photo: James R. Dean

In their early New York appearances their racial and structural oppositeness was constantly observed. It amuses Arnie that no one ever referred to him as a white person before he started working with Bill.

Arnie assisted Bill with the development of *Social Intercourse* in 1981; it was made on a shoestring budget, with volunteer dancing and singing by an ensemble including three of Jones' sisters, and costumed from thrift shops. They met Keith Haring at a college in Pennsylvania. Sensing a common impulse in their work, he designed a tee-shirt and poster for the production.

In his interview with Connie Kreemer, Bill talked about *Social Intercourse: Pilgrim's Progress*, which premiered at City Center, New York City, during 1981:

"For me, this piece was a turning point. It was my first foray into 'midtown dance,' a midtown venue, which says a lot about what I was trying to do and how I came equipped. It also indicated what I would be trying to do in the future and perhaps what I am doing now in a more refined way. I wanted to use pop imagery, so I chose three 'colored girl' singers—that's the generic term— because that's traditionally what you do when you want a 'hot' show. You get three singers who open their mouths and wail from deep within. I wanted them to sing things which were sentimental, like 'I Believe,' and I juxtaposed it with the most abrasive, ironic statement I could make about that quaint, seductive expression of faith.

"As the singers sang this beautiful song, the dancers did extremely hard-edged movement—bodyslapping, stomping on the floor. I also had overt images of sexual energy, people lying on each other kissing. There were a number of combinations and two or three times in the middle of a particularly active section, two men would come crashing mouth to mouth, kissing. One critic got upset and said, 'You only had to do that once, the shock value was there.' But it's beyond shock value, it's reality. This is our life style, it's real, it's an alternative life style; and this community, the company, represents a community which operates under rules which are sexual, racial, and class-stratified.

"We also wanted to pull in a broad audience and I think, in terms of a black community, we did that. More people came to see the piece because of its venue. I wanted to make something with a black voice, while I was trying to understand my own voice.

"I think of Chagall and his paintings, which are rich with imagery of Judaism, particularly the Russian Jews, and yet it is also
about painting as well as more universal things. I set out to do
that in this work. I wanted to make something which would exhaust
me. I wanted to make a mini-spectacle which had all the trappings
of a revue—one song, the song ends, there is a little interchange,
the dancers change costumes, another song, and the singers are
right there on stage with the microphones and musicians. It was
obviously entertainment, but challenging entertainment.

"It was the prototype for many things Arnie and I have been
trying to do. We want to make works that deeply affect people
and yet are cool and distant enough so that they can be observed
as a presence, appreciated for themselves and what they repre-
sent. This was our somewhat slick, midtown production. We realized that it wasn't as slick as it could be, but were trying to pull it
off at that level of the dance world. It was a very ambitious jump,
but it was also taking into account everything we'd been doing up
to that point and putting it together into an evening.

**Arnie photographing Bill
at the Kitchen** (1981)
photo: Paula Court

Social Intercourse:
Pilgrim's Progress (1981)
photo: Arnie Zane

Social Intercourse:
Pilgrim's Progress (1982)
Bill T. Jones and Rhonda
Moore
photo: Arnie Zane

"There were a lot of dancers in *Social Intercourse*. I used about 15 dancers plus a company of 5 or 6, which I had amassed especially for this piece.

"The opening section was the 'postmodern section.' When people came into the space, a guard was there and most of the dancers were moving back and forth in front of the theater door. We had an agreement with the house that we would never block the door, so when the guard said, 'Stop,' the dancers had to clear so that the people could walk to their seats.

"Apparently the guard said, 'Stop' in such an intimidating way that people thought, 'Oh, my God, once I get in there, I can't get out!' And that immediately made some people angry. They felt what I was doing was representing New York, the modern world, and what I was saying was that we're all trapped. I hadn't even thought of it in that way. I viewed it as a simple task, where the guard stopped the dancers so people could walk through, like a crosswalk, but people read metaphors and symbolism into it, just as in *Blauvelt Mountain*.

"In the next section, the structure was that the dancers were told to make a certain pass in a certain manner. They had to go from one side of the performing area to another, a certain number of times, and then change the quality of the way they did it. Then they were instructed to find partners and to continue this activity, stopping and going, at the command of one performer, another guard, until one by one, the couples lay down together and lay there on the floor on top of each other. Then the piece began.

"Many of these dancers were completely untrained, which was something I inherited from my early experimentation with dance making. This section was like the classic postmodern statements where anyone could dance, any two people could partner, any movement could follow any other movement. There was another section where these same dancers were used as a chorus for a production number that finished the first act. They came across the stage doing different motifs, and it kept on going, with very high energy, for the sheer spectacle of it.

"Many of us took the experimentations of Laura Dean and, maybe to a lesser degree, Lucinda Childs, to heart. This section was, in fact statements not so much about vocabulary, as about the way in which movement is perceived through time and space, and the way in which the energy level becomes an emotional, visceral response. In my own way, I was making that sort of task dance to see how much can be absorbed. That was the excitement for me. It was very raw, and it wanted to be what it represented, nothing else.

"*Social Intercourse* was a wild dance, designed to be all red and jagged and full of heart. The craft was secondary. The dance was bigger than we were. The dance was exhausting, but that's what it was about—pushing oneself to that limit, dealing with social issues of race, sexuality, and all those things.

"How was it a reflection of its culture? It's a complicated issue because it's dealing with the exchange between the artist and the artwork, the artwork and its audience. The work was a commentary on the way I perceived the society I was living in at that time. It was about the way I perceived the relationships between men and women and men and men, as well as the way I perceived the restraints. The kissing of the two men, crashing face against face, was intended, on one level, to break a barrier, to thumb one's nose, and, at the same time, to suggest the new world we're in, where anything is possible. We are living here now, that's what the work said. We have endless energy, and maybe we're a bit unpresentable, a bit raw, but here we are. Now you must deal with us.

"Concerning the exchange with the viewer, that would be determined by class, one's own particular background in modern dance and theater, one's race, and, perhaps sexual preference. All of those things would put the viewing in a certain relationship to that work.

"When I was choreographing, I never thought about it, in perhaps those terms, but I know the power in it. It's never that literal, it's like peripheral vision. I know one thing will produce a certain reaction. For example, the three 'colored girl' singers were up because I felt that black women are exploited. People say, 'Oh, they're so hot!'—which means they have a natural, uninhibited sensuality, which is what those people who don't have it want. The disco voice of the screaming Donna Summer or of the colored girls makes us think about sex, makes us feel alive, when we are not alive in that way. It's as if they were a symbol of colonialism or imperialism. Now, that's a pretty rarefied explanation for something which is that they basically provided the funk and were live singers who sang from a very natural place.

"The musicians were two white boys. Combined with the colored girls, it was truly an aesthetic melting pot, and it was a statement about the faith I had in lower Manhattan. It was an integrated cast dealing with the so-called emerging nations of the world (Harlem is an emerging nation) and it was a liberated vision of educated young people coming to power to make a new world which brings all cultures together into one new one. *Social Intercourse* questioned barriers between people. It was quite a responsibility to make dance about social statements, and yet, at the same time, it was full of ironies—like when the colored girl singers sang 'I Believe' while it was undercut with a dance about the death of belief."

—Connie Kreemer
Further Steps: Fifteen Choreographers On Modern Dance
June 5, 1984

Schooled in images and sound, experienced in the making of what might be called "kinetic cubism," they set about learning to work with music. Touring in Europe, they began meeting the seminal visual artists of their generation, inspiring and being inspired by them. Under the aegis of the Brooklyn Academy of Music's Next Wave Festival, they were attempting elaborate collaborations with other performers and designers. Throughout the early 1980s they worked separately, together, and with other choreographers. Arnie danced with Andy de Groat, perfecting a solo persona because he could not remember steps in ensemble work; the videotape recorder, which serves as an electronic memory, has made his intricate visual landscapes possible. They appeared in the works of Robert Longo. They were encouraged to explore fashion and technology onstage, along with their impulses to show and tell.

They felt pressured by the need to continually escalate the production values and scale of their pieces. Arnie observed that "for the past ten years, there has not been the luxury of time. The

Robert Longo's *Marble Fog* (1985) Arnie Zane, Adrienne Altenhaus, Sean Curran, at The Brooklyn Museum
photo: Paula Court

medium of dance turns in on itself. Before, people had lifetimes to create. We're not simply children of dance. We're information gatherers, processors, taking sustenance from a vast array of resources."

In 1983, Bill T. Jones/Arnie Zane & Co. achieved international acclaim with the premiere of *Intuitive Momentum* at the Brooklyn Academy of Music.

In *The Village Voice* Deborah Jowitt wrote: "In the beginning, the piece is kind of like a party, a testing of new relationships . . . . Jones and (Max) Roach, both, I think, improvising, have a high time stalking each other, waiting, pouncing, winding each other up . . . .

"The dancing is intense, rapid, high-spirited, not what you'd call easy-going. I always imagine that Jones and Zane have created an intricate patterned *thing* that they never quite show us the whole of. What we see is dancers slashing into part of that pattern, dropping through another, meeting each other in a third, pushing two parts of it so close together that the dancers' bodies have to overlap, deal with each other. Stamp, spin, pause a while, drop, kick, fast footwork, walk away. A lot of the movements are familiar, but the action is rarely predictable. What keeps the piece from being just a high-wattage display is a certain reassuring formality, the fact that you can see motifs repeated, varied, traded . . . . "

Intuitive Momentum
(1983) Bill T. Jones, Arnie
Zane, Max Roach
photos: Tom Caravaglia

Rotary Action (1984) background painting, *Tongue to the Heart*, by Robert Longo; Metro Pictures Gallery, NYC
photos: Paula Court

Robert Longo

O

Robert Longo
photo: Frank Ockenfels

"I met Bill and Arnie on tour in 1981, I'd *heard* of them: it seemed like there was some similarity. I'd seen a photograph of Bill that looked like my *Men in the Cities* drawings . . . . I took a workshop in contact improvisation. It was so boring . . . . I thought it would be like the music I was listening to, like the Sex Pistols, but instead it was so genteel . . . .

"I'm interested in physicality. It's the little nuances that bind me to their sensibility. I thought the best dancing was either sports or the way people died in movies. Bill and Arnie looked like a cross between sports and the Chinese ballet . . . . Bill was the average kind of person you'd expect to excel at this, but Arnie gave *me* this feeling that I could dance. Their vocabulary, the gestures, were on-line, hot wired . . . the same things I was talking about. I didn't see the structures; instead I constantly saw the picture. It was from a certain point of view; it was in a frame. The longer I watched, the more I started to understand their strategies . . . to deny virtuosity was like fucking around with the order at hand, operating within the structure, then destroying the structure, then rebuilding the structure. One day Bill gave me a sixty second history of dance.

"I was going to rock clubs and watching a band called the Contortions, which had random, psychotic impulses. I started to see those gestures in Bill and Arnie's work. A range of gestures, more than fashion, defines periods of time. There's a radical difference between the way Babe Ruth ran around the bases and the way people do it now, in the way Jesse Owens and Carl Lewis run. Gestures are very contemporary cultural indicators . . . . Did you ever see *El Topo?* A guy who has no legs and a guy who has no arms; one climbs on the other guy's back, and they become this giant. Bill and Arnie, when they want to, can become this superhuman being. They have a workmanlike quality, they're dancers, they do their job. I was real attracted to the high-level impact. Bill dives into Arnie's arms; they freeze and the lights go off—it's always a strategic kind of energy. I never liked watching them run around the stage; it was like wasting time. They were never trying to hide anything in the meaning of the work, but to constantly reveal or communicate.

"Another thing that attracted me to them is that the woman I live with, Gretchen, has done sets for them as well—she did a set for them in Paris—and we met as couples. There's this bonding . . . an interaction among four creative people, and the closeness can shift at any moment. There's a creative understanding. One quality they both have, that Gretchen and I have, is a kind of intense anger, and an overt gentleness. They're people I never want to have angry at me. In Paris, somebody was booing, and Bill ran off the stage after them.

"I've heard stories of their Binghamton days. I ended up in Buffalo the way they ended up in Binghamton. We were doing things in basically provincial locations; pursuing stuff on the frontier was always weird.

"When I worked with them on *Intuitive Momentum*, it was on *their* piece. I'm a total tyrant when it comes to my work. It's my ass on the line, and I'm totally responsible. They were clear; I basically delivered my aspect. I had to control myself and not get in the way of the performance. I wanted to light the set my way, but I had to acquiesce and let the lighting designer light the dances.

Inspiration (Two Moon July) (1984) documentary for Public Television on The Kitchen
photo: Paula Court

"You don't understand how they do it . . . . I'd been playing music with Rhys Chatham, and I'd seen Karole Armitage. I see the referential stuff in Bill and Arnie's work, but they're like flashes that located things you don't understand. History is like a weapon—a bullet you load into a gun, but you have to reinvent the gun . . . . There'll be this stuff going on, like people fucking, a fight, billboards for the Chinese ballet, some perverted Aztec symbol . . . . One of the things that aligns our sensibility is that we're not involved in pastiche. *Our* condition is more of collision, a cultural collision, wanting to see what will happen. You fuse things together. It has spontaneous elements, but the overall structure is intentional. It's not an open-ended kind of thing.

"Their dealing with the company is like my dealing with a lot of assistants. *Secret Pastures* was like reaching out beyond even what *they* wanted to do. I was afraid it would become associated with one particular artist's work, like Keith Haring's . . . . Bill's gestures opened up Keith's work. Bill and Arnie can locate themselves in the landscape between someone like Keith and someone like me, or Gretchen.

"The origin of it all is free . . . put together by a spirit, rather than a spirit generating it. It's real interesting to have friends that are makers—they function with a kind of spirituality that's above the daily activity of life, so there's a real strong camaraderie. It's fun to have someone to laugh with about your ambitions, and the fragility of being an artist. We're all so dependent on the support systems. The National Endowment for the Arts gave me grants for 'performance,' not for art; that really saved my ass.

"To be an artist is a perverse opportunity. You get a little crack in the fabric, and you turn it into a huge rip. Bill and Arnie have had to put a lot of trust in a lot of people to help them get their things going. I always had this naive idea that I'd just make my shit and give it to somebody to sell. Sometimes there are overlaps (in creative energy) with people in the business world, like Gretchen's brother Jonathan (who serves on Bill and Arnie's Board of Directors). We've all gotten older. We all watch each other's craft. I have become more of a director, and less of a painter. Bill and Arnie have helped me understand that that's OK—directing is an act of performance. It helped me to understand the role of a director as a critical performer. It was the first time I clearly related to them as performers. Arnie was always bitching about not wanting to be dancing. The love of the art form and of Bill kept Arnie dancing. In *Freedom of Information*, that was the first time someone took Arnie's moves, became his surrogate. The women in the company were these great amalgams of Bill and Arnie together. Then they brought in this guy, Sean Curran, who was really amazing, a poltergeist, this thing leaving this body and going into this other body. I associate these gestures very clearly with these people, and then they're, like, electronically transferred. It's a kind of physical envy; you long for it yourself. That's why sports are so important. Just imagine dunking a basket! You long to do these incredible gestures.

"But Bill and Arnie are not site-specific. I like the confusion their work creates gesturally—it isolates the act of motion. Drawing is a lot like walking. Motion is a lot like making—when you draw you make a motion. One of the strongest activities was that Bill did a solo, while Keith Haring painted a really fast mural in the background. A man and a landscape, happening at the same time. At The Kitchen, Bill exhausted several dancers; big doors would open and another guy would come out. They kept coming out through the doors.

"Arnie now is in a situation of the ultimate mysticism, hyperaware, hypersharp. In the most perverse way, I have a weird sense of jealousy of his condition. He's in a situation that's close to, that could be misconstrued as, sainthood. It's like Beethoven going deaf. There are natural geniuses and tortured geniuses . . . . The pieces are about torment, but the torment has so much to do with trying to understand. I watched Arnie watching a performance once; it was like leaving your body, hovering . . . . The work is fragmented now, but it's clearer.

"How artists can help each other is real critical; the currency that exists is inspiration. We influence each other. I've seen their effect on myself and Gretchen in the most positive ways. We make something in response to something we've seen them make, and vice versa. I've used Bill's face, screaming, and Arnie in a drawing. In *Killing Angels*, the choreography I created was meant to imitate their choreography. I associate a large piece, with several panels, to the way they choreograph something."

—**R. L.** (in conversation with Elizabeth Zimmer)
New York City, September 3, 1987

●

Gretchen Bender

○

"When Bill and Arnie approached me to collaborate with them on *Freedom of Information* I knew they understood my sensibility—the sensation that 'our insides are outside'—that the private self has become a public soul with denied responsibilities to its externalized psyche—a psyche that struggles with its awareness of loss of self. In *Freedom of Information*, Bill and Arnie's choreography moved with this knowledge and with the knowledge of being pawns in a culture of hidden agendas.

"In the first of the three sections, I wanted to reflect the electronic landscape I felt was the neighborhood of the gamelike violence of the choreography. David Cunningham's score greatly complemented the tone of the work, with the entrances and exits of my 'moving' set-design choreographed to the pacings of the score. The slide barrage designed for the end of Section I begins as the beat of the score starts to ominously churn and grind. As this happens, the dancers cool awareness of the cultural image-blitz directly mirrors my own feeling that society, instead of being overwhelmed, goes into overdrive in a complicated cultural environment.

Freedom of Information
photo: Paula Court

"For Section II, Bill and Arnie requested a sculptural element—Bill wanted a white wooden 'sandbox.' Because of the prohibitive heaviness, and the need to assemble and disassemble it in several minutes, we refined this idea into a 12' x 12' x 4' high skeletal aluminum cube that the dancers moved on and in and eventually upended.

"In Section III, choreographed strikingly by Arnie, I timed the 30 computer graphic abstractions I had created for the piece to occasionally appear and sweep across the full background. The sweep of the abstractions across the 'sky' every few minutes parallels the intrusive quality of the musical score at this point. The dancers move like rebellious computer chips beneath the black and white of the computer graphics film which projected the whole length and width of the stage—at least 20' high and 40' wide. As the music changes into a 'fascist' dance lesson, the dancers seem to rebel against the score. I introduced a sliding, zooming white filmic cube that joins in a playful, ambiguous rebellion as the dancers do. In fact, Arnie told me he choreographed this section to some Judy Garland show tunes—a perfect rebellion to the given score.

"As in any collaboration, the staging is where real compromises took place. Bill and Arnie were particularly flexible in accommodating a 'moving' set design. Their respect for my vision and their willingness to work creatively with the tech director in solving the lighting complexities of the piece, was of great value to me.

"I also realized a critical equation for the set design; that money and tech facilities at each venue are directly related to the quality of the film projection and, as Bill and Arnie taught me, one aspect of touring is about survival of the fittest sense of humor!

"The experience of collaborating with Bill and Arnie was exhilarating because all three levels—the dance, the music composition, and the set design—were allowed to cycle through a field of 'freedom of information.'

"By the end of 1984, I had developed an electronic performance genre—choreographing video on TV's in an architectural setting in black box theater. This 'media theater' work was directly inspired by my work with Bill T. Jones and Arnie Zane."

—G. B.
New York City, 1988

Gretchen Bender
photo: Frank Ockenfels

●

"Freedom of Information is also mystifying," wrote Alan M. Kriegsman in *The Washington Post* (1984). "The 'freedom' of the title is wildly uncontained, and 'information'—a multilayered barrage of imagery by turns violent and serene, erotic and playful, comical and ominous—comes at you in such swift, dense chunks that it's all but impossible to sort out as it's happening. Nonetheless, this postmodernist abstraction is as compelling as it is cryptic. Though the work seems urgently to want to 'mean' something—it's full of semantic cues, from the title to the text to the flux of relationships among the dancers—it resists any easy translation to literal terms. But viscerally and instinctively, one feels the absolute certainty and rigor of its conception. The thing flows with a mad logic of its own—*Freedom of Information* has in common with other powerful works of art that elusive quality of 'inevitability.'"

Freedom of Information
(1984) studio photograph
photo: Lois Greenfield

Freedom of Information, Section II (1984) Arnie Zane, Janet Lilly, Julie West, Amy Pivar, Poonie Dobson, Bill T. Jones; Saddler's Wells, England
photos: Peter Sayers

COFFEE
(Prologue to *Freedom of Information*)
Dancetext by Bill T. Jones

Mmmm, that's good, and that's why she called me on her birthday she didn't say what she was calling about she asked about myself. We posted these here missiles on them there hills. We posted them there missiles and they uh lined up for miles and miles we still posted them there missles.

She called me on her birthday—very charming I imagine what it was like when we were in Vienna in 1982 and we were eating linzer torte we posted those brochures and we talked to uh the Pope that day and he said come back next week and we were trying to get some hold on the corporate structure of the Vatican but she called me on her birthday and was very warm and talked about the flowers and the grachts in Amsterdam of all these wonderful things like the goats and the birds and the . . . . We posted these bullets that they were trying to sell somewhere in South America and it had something to do with the children being fed nestle's milk products and they were malnourished. She called me on her birthday and she said "How's your cup of coffee?" and I said, "Mmmm very good."

I remember walking the streets of London with her that day and she turned to me she was wearing a gingham dress or was it polka dots or it could have been moire silk or satin, she turned to me and said "Mmm how's your coffee?" I said, "We posted them there missiles, one there on that hill, we posted them there missiles and then we posted the bullets in South America too. She said, what was that little island called and I said I can't quite remember—it sounds like a coffee name.

Mmmm she called me on her birthday, she's German, she said "Would you like to dance?" I said "How?" She said "Hold up your right hand your right foot." And I held up my right, she said now shift your weight and I did, I stepped like so and like so . . . . She said, "Mmmm, that's good." And I moved my hips this way and I moved my hips that way and she said, "Do you have anything?" I said, "What do you mean?" " . . . You know, in case." We posted them there missiles over there on that hill. We posted them there missiles on that little island, just like cof-

Freedom of Information
(1984) studio photograph
photo: Lois Greenfield

fee . . . she said, "Mmmm," that day in London, we went to the museum and there were those stones that the Greek people are trying to get back again. We went to that there museum she said "Lift up your right hand" I lifted up my left she said "Lift up your right foot" I shifted my weight into my right hip and then into my left, she said "Mmmm, that's good, she said mmm, that real good, she said "Shall we dance" and then we began to turn, she said "let me see your profile" I said I love to have my picture taken she said do you like to be taken I said it depends on where I'm going.

Mmmm, how's your cup of coffee? I said the light is in my eyes and she said do you like my dress and I said no I don't like your dress I like you without it she said do you have anything I said what do you mean she said you know, do you have anything in case I shifted my weight into my right leg and then shifted back into the left and she said mmm, that's good, she said mmm, that's real good she said lift up your hands and I lifted up both hands she said now drop your head and I lifted my chin she said show me your dancing and I put these together like so and then those there and then here and there and then the music swelled and I was doing it faster than I had ever done it before she said mmm, that's good, do you have anything—I said what do you mean— she said you know in case and then over there we posted them there missiles on that hill and he didn't care they lined up for miles and miles she said you know in case—lift up your right hand lift up your left hand. I said Mmm, that's good.

And we posted them there missiles on them there hills, and we posted them there missiles, and he didn't give one good god damn what happened to them there people on that little island. "Hold up your right hand. Hold up your left. Mmmm, that's good."

Secret Pastures (1983)
Duet at the Paula Cooper
Gallery
photo: Arnold Wengrow

Secret Pastures (1984)
photo: Tom Caravaglia

Secret Pastures (1984)
photos: Paula Court

"*Secret Pastures* may be the first dance work of any conse-
quence to acknowledge the influence of MTV on our perception;
. . . the scenario, like many for MTV is wholeheartedly absurd—I
don't wonder why Zane is cast as an eccentric scientist, Jones as
'The Fabricated Man,' half the talented cast as various urban
types, and the other half (we're told) as 'purely imaginary.' The
plot concerns the choosing of personnel for a scientific expedition
to a newly discovered island, work and play on the island (including an encounter with some monkeys with hair in cute places, and
an orgy), a near disaster for the Scientist, and the departure, with
the Fabricated Man—abandoned by the society he had tried to
join—alone in the denuded structure of the expedition tent.

"Jones and Zane have chosen their collaborators astutely. Marcel Fieve has given the dancers up-to-the-minute hair styles, cut
and slanted and colored ornately. Willi Smith's costumes range
from urban outrage to Banana Republic chic to dazzling Milliskin
with chunks cut out (these last the only ones I didn't admire). Zane,
for instance, scuttles about with a loose, billowing, pale colored
robe over his shirt and pants, sporting glasses and what looks like
a tall blond mohawk over his own short dark hair.

"Peter Gordon's stupendous score is eclectic in the way that
Jones and Zane's choreography is. The latter transform a lot of
the movement of the day and mix it with their own abrasive
angular gestures, spins and leaps and high legwork, disco raunch.
Contact Improvisation's unusual lifts live in a harmony of sorts.
Jones and Zane even capitalize on Sean Curran's skill at Irish
stepdancing in a knockout little solo that doesn't seem at all out of
place. Gordon is equally skilled at stylistic incongruities that blend
into a unified whole . . . . "

—**Deborah Jowitt**
The Village Voice, 1984

Secret Pastures (1984)
photos: Tom Caravaglia

Bill T. Jones, body painted
by Keith Haring,
photographed by Tseng
Kwong Chi

**Study for Fabricated Man
Costume**
photo: Tseng Kwong Chi

Keith Haring
photo: Paula Court

Keith Haring met Bill and Arnie by accident, through a friend in Kutztown, Pennsylvania. First he drew a poster for them. "Then I painted while Bill danced, at The Kitchen. Then they asked me to do the sets for *Secret Pastures*. It's about just talking, getting ideas back and forth, conversations that have nothing to do with the dance or the piece at hand. Productive conversations about anything. Things happen without your forcing them to happen, with very little effort. It's a lot easier to work with someone you can understand, who's had similar experiences, similar views about life. Painting Bill, in 1983, was the first time I painted an entire body. He knew what to do with the body after it was painted. He made it work in a whole other way. Since 1984, I've painted Grace Jones four times."

Bill T. Jones, body painted by Keith Haring, photographed by Tseng Kwong Chi

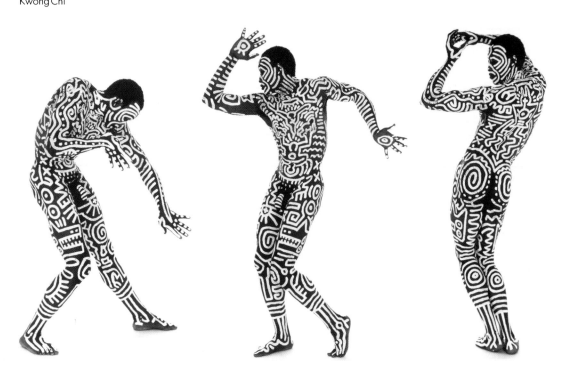

In a 1988 interview with Cathy Lichtman for *City Arts*, Bill recalled the creative atmosphere that helped to produce 1984's *Secret Pastures*:

"When we made *Secret Pastures* we were thinking about how we could make something that would be happy and yet people in the know, the downtown dance scene, would recognize that underneath it was a post-modern exercise in dance in many of the same ways that we make dance now. If you stripped the costumes off and looked at these groups of patterns and the things we were doing, it was very abstract. It was a very slight story. It was an excuse for a lot of dancing. At that time we were very interested in the downtown scene, and how the high art and the low art worlds came together. I can remember being at an opening of Keith Haring's a few years ago where there would be some very chic collector from Basel, Switzerland, and Bianca Jagger, and over in the corner there's break dancers and there's Andy Warhol over here and then there's probably a young investment banker here and a museum curator there. This was the scene. And these people came to Secret Pastures. They definitely came around Keith's involvement. We wanted that melange."

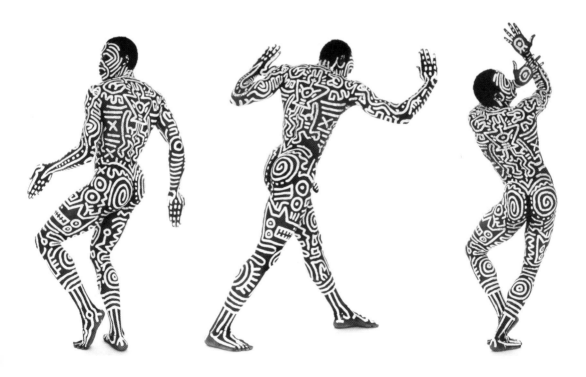

Peter Gordon   ○

Peter Gordon
photo: Paula Court

"I first began working with Bill and Arnie in early 1982, when they were preparing a new duet for the Vienna Dance Festival. There was no time to compose a new work, so we spent a day in my studio, listening to tapes of music already recorded. They would describe what would happen in each section and I would find an excerpt which seemed to complement the dance. Using six different selections we assembled a twenty minute tape suite which became the score for *Rotary Action*. During this process, we found we had much in common with regard to attitude, irony, sense of flow and a desire for sensual answers to formal questions. Our next work together was *Fever Swamp*, a dance commissioned for the Alvin Ailey Company which used as its score an earlier work of mine, *Intervallic Expansion*. After they discovered they like the 'musical' aspects of the work (sound, feel, beat) they became very interested in the structure of the piece. In the music, the melodic, rhythmic, and harmonic aspects are all based on the concept of singular elements expanding, increasing in number and interacting in more complex ways over time. The resulting dance included many of these musical ideas within their very unique choreographic approach.

"During the following summer of 1983, I spent two months in Ireland with video artist Kit Fitzgerald, working on the video/music pastoral, *Return of the Native*. We invited Bill and Arnie to spend a number of days with us and appear as characters in the landscape. In the intense period of working and living together on the tip of County Kerry's Dingle peninsula, we began discussions about a full evening work for the Brooklyn Academy of Music, which would become *Secret Pastures*. The work would involve a journey through a number of different fictional geographies. The dance and the music would work as parallel entities, sometimes in unison, sometimes contrapuntally. As the piece evolved over the next year, they would hear some of the music before they choreographed the dance, other music would be composed after I had seen some choreography and still other sections would have the music and the choreography completed concurrently, without seeing what the other was doing. It was almost uncanny how timings and phrasings would almost always work perfectly together, even when we were working separately. Initially I would prepare some rough sketch tapes for them. Then, two weeks before the opening, I would rehearse daily with them and my ensemble of a dozen musicians. It was during this period that the music and dance would come alive and become one. Up until now, all of our collaborations had been with tape music, but having the dancers in the same room with the musicians for so long allowed for a type of telepathy to transpire which musicians or dancers usually find only among themselves. I found working on *Secret Pastures* to be totally invigorating artistically because I was inspired to create music quite different to what I might have done if left totally to my own devices, yet at the same time so natural and personal that now I don't see how I could have written anything else. Even though a collaboration is often a rocky road, I value as most important the friendship which developed over the years of working together."

–P. G.
Brooklyn, 1987

•

Secret Pastures (1984)
Collaborators Peter Gordon,
Bill T. Jones, Arnie Zane,
Keith Haring, Willi Smith
photo: Paula Court

Bill has felt himself driven to "a kind of dance-making that took me away from my earlier impulses, the desire to tell a story or present an autobiographical bit of sound commentary. *The Animal Trilogy* was arbitrary, completely self-referential, a pure abstraction."

"You know," said Bill in an interview with Cathy Lichtman (*City Arts*, 1988), "I always want to prepare people for the work, how to look at it. We're really not about lyrical dancing at all, and that's a hard thing for people to understand. The work feels very cerebral when you're watching it. I read a review from Ann Arbor about 'Elephant,' that said it seemed to be a display of abstract movement for the sake of abstract movement. Quite frankly, it was. It is as abstract as Mondrian sitting and playing with his grids, as abstract as Picasso or Braque dealing with planes in a painting. I am obsessed with how one movement just butts against another one. Lyrical transitions are really not part of it right now.

"Its just like Louise Nevelson. Finding something and putting it into your painting. We're very influenced by the visual arts. Some people might say, 'Those rules don't apply in performance because we want continuity; we want human qualities; we want a subtext; we want an experience that we can identify with.' And sometimes, this is really not there.

"Right now I'm not even so concerned with totality of structure because I actually believe in ways similar to Merce [Cunningham], that in a performance, you really only go from moment to moment."

The Animal Trilogy (1986)
studio photograph, Vernon
Sharpe, Janet Lilly, Sean
Curran, Heywood McGriff, Jr.
photo: Lois Greenfield

"*History of Collage*, our first collaboration," Bill said, "was created in spite of our shared resolution to work apart in Arnie's last year of life. Old patterns are not easily left behind. After witnessing a sequence of mine that took place at the end of a fruitful rehearsal, Arnie was inspired to 'take off' from some of my ideas. I then repaid the compliment, and soon a new work—dreamlike, rambling, yet compelling—was taking shape. Because of everpresent financial restraints we asked the dancers to empty their closets for costumes. Charles Amirkhanian and 'Blue' Gene Tyrrany generously provided us with a score, and as is often the case Robert Wierzel gave us elegant lighting and décor that was as effective as it was inexpensive."

The History of Collage
(1988) Arthur Aviles,
Lawrence Goldhuber
photo: Tom Brazil

The History of Collage
(1988) Sean Curran, Demian
Acquavella, Janet Lilly,
Arthur Aviles
photo: Tom Brazil

Bill said: "*Fever Swamp* was intended as a 'suit of clothes' made specifcally for the Ailey Company. It was designed to be formal romp. It was to be like running a four-minute mile—the smartest pop work I could conceive. The title was taken from one of the most negative reviews I had ever gotten, accusing me of 'leading a generation into the *fever swamps*.' This was a term I had never heard but one that I was willing to take as a challenge: How to make a work with all the formal invention and conviction of any of our earlier experiments and at the same time have new life, color and popular appeal. The fact that all six men were black made the experiment very special and exciting for me.

"Both Arnie and I found outlets for our individual efforts as choreographers. We both insisted on the support of the other in whatever we undertook; however, the circumstances of our working alone often contained some painful contrasts. I was offered commissions and opportunities that were not available to him. *Fever Swamp* is an example. We struggled to be seen as co-choreographers, rather than my being choreographer and his being business manager and choreographic assistant. The opportunity for us to work independently, free of the other's immediate impulse, was at this point a very welcome and fruitful challenge."

Fever Swamp (1983) Alvin Ailey American Dance Theater
photo: Perry Adleman

Fever Swamp (1983) studio
photograph, Bill T. Jones,
Janet Lilly, Sean Curran
photo: Lois Greenfield

Bill, Arnie, Alvin Ailey
photo: Susan Kuklin

Both men are relieved and gratified by the new work they are doing, separately, together, and in collaboration with their young company. Bill describes Arnie's new quartet, *The Gift/No God Logic*, as "beautiful . . . it breathes the way humans breathe. For Arnie this piece came as a burst 'away' from the stricture of our shared choreographic pressure and 'toward' a deeper understanding of his own agenda as dance maker/artist. Here he could exercise his penchant for tableaux and sculptural repetitions. (In a sense this is the other side of collaborations: the space that opens up for us to discover, by contrast, what is truly our own.) This particular work was a 'gift'on two levels at once—an offering to two dear friends, Herbert and Nadine Lust, and also a special delivery package for the world. For the man losing strength daily there was no God-derived logic."

The Gift/No God Logic
(1988) Arthur Aviles, Heidi Latsky, Demian Acquavella
photo: Lois Greenfield

"To me, this is the strongest of Zane's last works," writes Deborah Jowitt (*The Village Voice*, 1988). "The pristine maneuvers of four dancers almost always occur within, or in relation to, a clump or a line. An autonomous world. In one formation to which they keep returning, they face in different directions, as if on watch for trouble coming from afar; and, except for a brief flurry of hostility, each seems vigilant to maintain the group's harmony and equilibrium, to lift the fallen, or lean over that someone else may climb onto that bent back. The four dancers move gravely from one position to another, their control and steadfastness a poignant contrast to the soaring soprano arias from Verdi's *La Forza del Destino*."

The Gift/No God Logic
(1988) Arthur Aviles, Demian Acquavella, Heidi Latsky, Sean Curran
photo: Lois Greenfield

During the '60s and '70s powerful social forces—liberation movements, a strong economy which supported the arts, free public education and the opportunity for geographic and economic mobility it provides—helped to produce the phenomenon of Bill T. Jones/Arnie Zane & Company, and the larger phenomenon of the personal relationship between two men that began in 1971. It has taken the 1980's—Reaganomics, AIDS, the "dumbing down" of American cultural life—to threaten every aspect of their art and their relationship.

Bill T. Jones and Arnie Zane have been better equipped than some of their colleagues to survive transitions in American taste. From the jump, Bill has understood that his chance for success lay on a platform, either a stage or a pulpit. For years, Arnie has had his heart set on directing and choreographing a Broadway musical. Their astonishing collaboration was hatched in a minimalist, populist period in American dance theater, and took advantage of the new license to mix media and mode. It has come of age in a time of almost unprecedented greed and social disregard. Their talent is such that they both seduce and bait their audience, entertain and teach, amuse and terrify. They are consummate collaborators, with each other and a host of other American artists. They are highly intelligent, verbal, gifted individuals, with a thorough understanding of their profession and the economic and political forces that play upon it. In 1986 they received a Bessie—a New York Dance and Performance Award—which cited them "for a dramatic retrospective whose conceptual scope and peerless dancing—from the solos to *Freedom of Information*—fully confirm a unique artistic partnership." Their company, which has had as many as eleven dancers, has appeared in twenty-five states and twenty-two countries, and on film and television.

But it is 1988. The building in Binghamton that housed the American Dance Asylum, which they helped to found, is now the Whitney Center for Dance, run by a ballet teacher. The nature of the Jones – Zane collaboration is changing. Bill says he now collaborates primarily with the other members of the company.

They continue working, driving in from Rockland County to choreograph and rehearse the company, preparing for the 1988 season at City Center. Arnie's most recent work, critics generally agree, may well be his strongest. "After so many years, I saw that if I was selfish, didn't listen to Bill, the ring of the work was much more distinctly mine. I've gotten a great pleasure, recently, out of working alone. At 38, it's about time to make the music and the steps work together."

"We've gone from being a very raw to a very cleaned-up act; we're now trying to infuse our marginality with the craft. I want to retain and be proud of the marginality, and also to appropriate the qualities of expert technical dancing. I've come to see the making of art as getting ideas out there, ideas about the human condition. I'm tired of seeing gay men choreographing a heterosexualized ideal situation of princesses."

As this essay is written, he is at work on *Like in Egypt*, a work which "has a degree of whimsy in it, a child's knowledge" of the Egyptian aesthetic. "My subconscious is a pot of soup, full of Hollywood and four years of studying art history at a university. I'm not looking for authenticity."

Each in his own way, these two men have gone to an edge, looked over, learned, and returned home. they have enlarged their circle of creative partners, while building an ensemble of performers equal to the theatrical and physical demands they make. Their community includes visual artists as well as dancers; they are savvy about markets and media as well as transparent to their respective muses.

This volume documents the story so far of a pair of careers. It illustrates a very American story, in poetry, prose, photography, and the naked data of a choreographic chronology. It represents a beginning.

Johnson City (1972)
photo: Arnie Zane

**Bill and Arnie with
Company in residence in
Richmond, Virginia
(1986)**
photo: Richmond Newspapers

21 Supported Positions
photos: Frank Ockenfels

Afterwords

Arnie Zane died of AIDS-related lymphoma on March 30, 1988 at the home he and Bill shared in Valley Cottage. His last performance, in a cameo role, took place on January 30 at the Ohio Theater, Cleveland, Ohio in what was to be the final collaboration of Bill T. Jones and Arnie Zane, *The History of Collage*.

Bill T. Jones/Arnie Zane & Co., now under the sole artistic directorship of Bill T. Jones, continues as a memorial to Arnie Zane. Future projects of the company include *The Last Supper at Uncle Tom's Cabin, Featuring 52 Handsome Nudes*, a project Arnie was developing from his hospital bed during the last two month of his life. The work will make use of a found-photo essay Zane assembled some years earlier, entitled *Negroes for Sale*. Likewise, there is *Lament*, a work using the text of Jenny Holzer. Arnie conceived this piece's central image as himself standing on an oversized table and chair shouting a Japanese lesson instructed by choreographer Ruby Shang.

Bill continues to choreograph and dance, feeling that his artistic sensibility is now as near an amalgam of his and Arnie's as can be considered possible. He believes that all new work must look forward and backward simultaneously: forward in order to search and grow, backward for encouragement, comparison and continuity.

In *High Performance* (1987), Ann Daly writes, "Though in a more stylistic than technical way, Bill T. Jones and Arnie Zane have also combined genres to come up with something of their own. With backgrounds in athletics and photography, Jones and Zane were seen by some as having sold out their renegade roots for the big time when they blatantly exploited the trappings of ballet in *Secret Pastures*, their contribution to the 1984 Next Wave Festival. But I think that Jones and Zane have done the most thorough and creative job of completely transforming ballet—as well as jazz, gymnastics, social dance, sports, folk dance and vernacular gesture—into their own pastiched style. Not only do they mix movement vocabularies but choreographic quotations and cross-genre witticisms as well in *The Animal Trilogy*, Jones and Zane made facile references to Ballanchine, Cunningham and Graham, continuing their interest in filmic techniques, the choreographers created a processional entrance which immediately 'rewound' itself, like a film run backward. Whereas Fenley's and Dean's dances were undermined by the classical sheen, Jones and Zane are in complete control of their variegated material.

"And through the persistence of their own fanciful ideas, they have been able to deal unabashedly with the virtuosity of their company's dancing without needing the rhetoric of classicism to justify it. The dancers pack these disparate steps together with utmost clarity and invest them with all-out exuberance. There is no mistaking these explosive contemporary dancers—despite their balletic carriage and *ballon*—for 'proper' classical dancers."

Like in Egypt (1988) Arthur
Aviles, Demian Acquavella,
Sean Curran
photo: Kenneth J. Cooper

"Zane built his dances with a photographer's eye for the telling prose, the uncluttered line; a dance minimalist's relish of repetition and subtle, brainy variation; a personal preference for punchy, succinct movement; and a love of 'style' and stylishness. *Like in Egypt* is a trio for Acquavella, Aviles and Curran—a series of carefully controlled power plays, with solos and encounters bursting in and out of eccentrically archaic frieze dances."

—**Deborah Jowitt**
The Village Voice, 1988

In an interview with Janice Berman (*New York Newsday,* July 22, 1988), Jones said: "This company is the child that Arnie and I had. In terms of unions, that's some product . . . . It was 17 years of work and a dream which he loved incredibly. He didn't say I *had* to keep it going, but I think as a challenge to myself, as a memorial to him, it's important that I do keep the company together. I love this group of people . . . .

"[Since Zane's death, the company is] much more committed . . . . They're very good people. The company knows just how fragile this enterprise is that we're undertaking, and they really pull together. The group is much more mature now. They were all there when Arnie died.

"I can see his hand in my choreography. I subconsciously began to take on some of his ways of working. So, yes, stylistically I've absorbed those things. But I am Bill, I'm not Arnie, and I'm not Bill and Arnie, which was a hard thing to realize. So I'm going deeper into myself, into my tastes. I have to trust them a bit more."

Absence(1989)
photos: Johan Elbers

The Daily Fact of Absence
Burt Supree

Bill T. Jones and Arnie Zane were an unlikely pair if you think couples are supposed to match. Their long-term relationship—as men working together—was central to the duets they first became noted for, that so oddly and uncompromisingly balanced challenge and cooperation. Zane was abrupt in moving, outspoken, a note taker, a business head, a photographer; Jones was a fierce, silky, natural dancer, a warrior, an intuitive force. Both could be physically explosive, though onstage Jones was more emotionally volatile, and, like some people who are astonishingly beautiful, was comfortable with the power his charm exerted.

When Zane got sick, they kept working and touring, and he participated as much as he was able to. A year ago, Zane made *The Gift/No God Logic*. When he choreographed it he was feeling rotten and thinking it might be the last dance he'd ever make. "I felt I was living in a devastating world I wasn't able to control," he told me last January. Countering that, *The Gift* is a sober, eloquent work, full of strangeness and mutual support.

Jones insists, "Arnie never felt he had made any piece about AIDS," and Zane would have hated having *The Gift* seen narrowly as a reaction to his illness. But in *The Gift* he made a piece that, without ever getting literal or preachy, consciously tried to set the world aright, to restore the values and balance that were missing.

Wrestling with Zane's illness forced them to reassess their work as well as their lives. "Our whole chemistry was changed," says Jones. Suddenly, there was no time for doing things you don't mean. "I'd thought I wanted a very sleek, modern dance company," said Zane. But having achieved that, they found themselves looking back to rediscover what had given a piece like *Blauvelt Mountain*—the 1979 duet that was their favorite—its substance and emotional resonance.

"We'd gotten involved in large spectacles with incredible energy, glittering, smashing to the eye," says Jones. "Then economy and directness became important. We wanted the company to feel what we had felt when we had nothing to lose and did things close to the bone. We asked for more of themselves. And I wanted to reassure myself of community—not just to be part of a high-powered, high-finance, high-visibility dance world.

"We knew we couldn't go home again, like when I was doing those early talking solos or we rolled around on the floor. We were working with people different from us, and now there was more at stake. There's the company and the pressure of maintaining it. If the company doesn't make money, you lose the company, you lose the *health insurance*. The company gives us life: I like that thought."

The last work they did together, *The History of Collage*, started out as a rumination on art history but acquired a political face. When they added the soundtrack ("Blue" Gene Tyranny's *White Night Riot*, built on sounds from the night the Dan White verdict came down in San Francisco) they realized that its power colored everything. "It could be a statement on sexuality just by virtue of the way we costumed the piece. We gave the men and women in the company the freedom to dress themselves as flamboyantly as they wanted."

What Jones and Zane brought to their duets was the full roominess and flexibility of their relationship: their daring, skill, playfulness; their willingness to pit themselves against each other, to attack or support each other; their ability to share. Without proclaiming intimacies, the facts of their relationship were put onstage in the play of weight and balance, of aggression and dependency. As gay men, they didn't flaunt a lifestyle, they didn't make a programmatic call to arms or plea for understanding, they didn't yearn for romance. They simply refused to pretend or apologize. Their private lives remained nobody's business. But they built their dances on the difference of character and physicality inherent in their relationship. That was right up front. Some audiences were flustered, but most responded to the immediacy and authority of the work. Dance—theirs and others'—is transforming awareness. That men who are not brothers or teammates may deeply care about each other is permanently in our consciousness.

In his short solo *Red Room*, made last summer while Zane was still living, Jones "tried to encapsulate where I was at then. It's a kind of anthem to loneliness, struggle, beauty." A strong puzzling piece, *Red Room* is full of strange flashes and contradictions: Jones meant it to contain everything of that moment in his life when it was made.

Red Room (1987)
photo: Frank Ockenfels

"I never make overtly dramatic movement. My concerns in my own dancing are about a kind of neoclassical plastique—to explore my physicality, to sculpt my body as an object. But the movement had feeling to me and I let my heart and anger color it from performance to performance. Doing it, I never felt so close to jazz before. The timelessness of love and grief—that's what I charge it with."

Now Jones is preparing a piece called *Absence*, set to the Berlioz song from his cycle *Les Nuits d'ete*. It's full of the imagery of loss, but, says Jones, "I was working on it long before Arnie died. The dancers are topless, dressed in sheets, with their backs to the audience. We had all these sheets we took from Roosevelt Hospital—the nurses encouraged us. We had enough for a month, but Arnie died four days later. Not a lot happens, but it's quite grand. Maybe its something metaphysical. I don't know. I'm thinking, what if there's another world? Who are his companions now?"

After long illness and the indignities of physical deterioration, the death of one's companion from AIDS doesn't come as a surprise. The shared battle draws a couple closer and closer—and then one partner exits. Nothing prepares one for the daily fact of that absence—for all the things that are absolutely missing, for all the questions that find no response, for the reams of confusing paperwork—mysterious medical bills, tax returns—that continue to miraculously proliferate, for the erratic bouts of rage and misery.

In dancing, "I'm trying to look at my personal style, to fill my work with all my passion and feeling," but, at the same time to let it be "abstract enough so people can get into it. It's got to include all aspects of my experience—grief, loss, the bitterness of premature death." But, almost by definition, the things that make life precious must be there too in force.

"I look closely at my body and its energy. I've been making long sequences of movements that refer to or are drawn from emotional states—though an outsider probably couldn't tell—and I dance them to many kinds of music, to learn all they can tell me about feeling and movement.

"There's no morality in the universe; there is no fairness. I've always tried to address the ugliest feelings—like feelings of oppression—and tried to transform them. I'm filled with anger and awareness of mortality and I want that to show.

"How much time do any of us have left? I don't know. The stakes have been raised in our rush to the finish line."

—B. S.
The Village Voice, June 28, 1988

D-Man in the Waters
(1989) Bill T. Jones, Arthur
Aviles
photo: Lois Greenfield

Chronology of Premieres: 1971–89

COLLABORATIONS	FIRST PERFORMED
1973 **Pas de Deux for Two** Music: Benny Goodman	137 Washington Street Binghamton, New York
1974 **Dances for a Third American Century** Performed by 25 dancers Collaboration with Lois Welk	Albany, Stony Brook, Warwick, New York
1975 **Dancing and Video in Binghamton** Collaboration with Meryl Blackman Performed by 8 dancers	Experimental Television Center, Binghamton, New York
1975 **Across the Street** Text: Bill T. Jones Film: Arnie Zane	American Dance Asylum Binghamton, New York
1978 **Whosedebabedoll? Baby Doll** Text: Bill T. Jones and Arnie Zane	American Dance Asylum Binghamton, New York
1979 **Monkey Run Road** Music: Helen Thorington Set & Costumes: Bill T. Jones and Arnie Zane Text: Bill T. Jones	American Dance Asylum Binghamton, New York
1980 **Sweeps** Video: Meryl Blackman Painting: Rosina Kuhn	Zurich, Switzerland
1980 **Blauvelt Mountain** Music: Helen Thorington Set: Bill Katz Lighting: William Yehle	Dance Theater Workshop New York City
1981 **Valley Cottage** Music: Helen Thorington Set: Bill Katz Lighting: William Yehle Text: Bill T. Jones and Arnie Zane Slides: Arnie Zane	Dance Theater Workshop New York City

1982	**Rotary Action** Music: Peter Gordon Lights: William Yehle	New Dance, NYC Vienna Festival Vienna, Austria
1982	**Dance for the Convergence of Three Rivers** Music by George Lewis	Three Rivers Arts Festival Pittsburgh, Pennsylvania
1983	**Intuitive Momentum** Music: Max Roach and Connie Crothers Set: Robert Longo Costumes: Ronald Kolodzie Lighting: Craig Miller Performed by 5 dancers	Brooklyn Academy of Music Brooklyn, New York
1984	**Freedom of Information** Music: David Cunningham Set and Visuals: Gretchen Bender Spoken Text: Bill T. Jones Lighting: William DeMull Performed by 6 Dancers	Theatre de la Ville Paris
1984	**Secret Pastures** Music: Peter Gordon Sets: Keith Haring Costumes: Willi Smith Lighting: Stan Pressner Hair, Makeup, and Painting of Fabricated Man Costume: Marcel Fieve Performed by 13 dancers	Brooklyn Academy of Music Brooklyn, New York
1986	**The Animal Trilogy** Music: Conlon Nancarrow Sets: Cletus Johnson Costumes: Bill Katz Lighting: Robert Wierzel Additional Set Elements for Part 3 by Tony Smith	Biennale Internationale de la Danse Lyon, France Commissioned in part by the Brooklyn Academy of Music, where it was later performed

**Marcel Fieve with Arnie
Zane** (1984)
photo: Paula Court

1987   **Where the Queen Stands
        Guard**
        Music: **Verdiana** by Vittorio
            Rieti, performed by the St.
            Lukes Chamber Ensemble
        Set and costumes: Frank L.
            Viner
        Lighting: Robert Wierzel
        Performed by 11 dancers

Triplex Theater
Borough of Manhattan
    Community College
New York City
Commissioned by St. Lukes'
Chamber Ensemble

1988   **The History of Collage**
        Music: Charles R.
        Amirkhanian,
        "Blue" Gene Tyranny

Cleveland, Ohio

**Where the Queen Stands
Guard** (1987) Lawrence
Goldhuber, Heywood
McGriff, Jr.
photo: Lois Greenfield

CHOREOGRAPHY: BILL T. JONES   FIRST PERFORMED

1974	**A Dance with Durga Devi** Music: Tibetan Temple Chants and Bessie Smith	American Dance Asylum Binghamton, New York
1974	**Negroes for Sale** Tape Collage: Bill T. Jones Visuals: Arnie Zane	Collective for Living Cinema New York City
1974	**Entrances** Performed by 4 dancers	American Dance Asylum Binghamton, New York
1974	**Track Dance** Set: Don Bosch Music: Lou Grassi Performed by 50 dancers	SUNY Binghamton Binghamton, New York
1975	**Could be Dance**	American Dance Asylum Binghamton, New York
1975	**Across the Street There Is a** **Highway** Performed by 28 dancers, including many Jones family members	The Farm San Francisco, California
1975	**Woman in Drought**	American Dance Asylum Binghamton, New York
1975	**Impersonations**	American Dance Asylum Binghamton, New York
1975	**Everybody Works/All Beasts** **Count** Music: a capella duet by Arnie Zane and Linda Berry with 14 dancers	Ensemble Performance at American Dance Asylum Solo Performance at Clark Center, New York City
1977	**For You**	Daniel Nagrin Dance Theatre New York City
1977	**Stomps**	Daniel Nagrin Dance Theatre New York City
1977	**Walk**	Daniel Nagrin Dance Theatre New York City
1977	**A Man**	Daniel Nagrin Dance Theatre New York City

Everybody Works (1976)
solo performance, The Clark
Center, New York City
photo: Nathaniel Tileston

1977	**Asymmetry: Every Which Way** Music: Lou Grassi visuals: Bill T. Jones and Peer Bode Enacted by 6 performers	Roberson Art Center Sears Harkness Theatre Binghamton, New York
1977	**Da Sweet Streak Ta Love Land** Music: Otis Redding Mask: Bill T. Jones Performed by 6 dancers	Clark Center New York City
1978	**Floating the Tongue** Solo improvisation in four phases	Kent School for Boys Kent, Connecticut Shown at The Kitchen, New York City, 1979
1978	**Naming Things is Only the Intention to Make Things** Duet with Jazz vocalist Jeanne Lee Text and Costumes: Bill T. Jones	The Kitchen New York City
1978	**Progresso** Set: Bill T. Jones	The Kitchen New York City
1978	**By The Water** Duet performance with Sheryl Sutton Set Construction: Charles Kiesling in collaboration with Sheryl Sutton and Bill T. Jones	American Dance Asylum Binghamton, New York
1979	**Echo** Music: Helen Thorington	The Kitchen New York City
1979	**Addition** Lighting: Carol Mullins	Washington Square Church New York City
1979	**Circle in Distance** Text and Movement in collaboration with Sheryl Sutton Set arranged by Bill T. Jones and Sheryl Sutton Lighting: Carol Mullins	Washington Square Church New York City

Circle in Distance (1979)
Bill T. Jones and Sheryl Sutton
photo: Arnie Zane

1980   **Dance in the Trees**   Hartman Land Reserve
Environmental work for 10   Cedar Falls, Iowa
community people and 2
musicians
Music: Jeff Cohan and Pete
Simonson
Costumes: Renata Sack and
Bill T. Jones

1980   **Open Places: A Dance in**   Waterloo, Iowa
June
Environmental work for 21
adults and children
performed in four park
settings
Music: Dan Hummel, Mark
Gaurmond, Thomas Berry
Costumes: Renata Sack and
Bill T. Jones

1980   **Untitled Duet**   Recreation Center
With Serry Satenstrom   Waterloo, Iowa
Music: Dan Hummell, Marcia
Miget, and Dartanyan
Brown

1980   **Balancing the World**   University of Northern Iowa
Performed as a duet with   Cedar Falls, Iowa
Julie West   Amerika House, Berlin
Lighting: William Yehle
Performed by 6 dancers

1980   **Sisyphus**   Terrace Theater
Music: Helen Thorington   Kennedy Center
Text: Bill T. Jones   Washington, D.C.
Set: Bill T. Jones

1981   **Judgment**   California Institute of the Arts
(solo with tape recorder)   Valencia, California

1981   **Social Intercourse: Pilgrim's**   Stewart Theatre
Progress   American Dance Festival
Assisted by Arnie Zane   Duke University
Music: Joe Hannon   Raleigh, North Carolina
Text and Lyrics: Bill T. Jones   (5 dancers)
Additional material   Later performed at The
composed and sung by   Space at City Center
Johari Briggs, Rhodessa   New York City,
Jones and Flo Brown   by 18 dancers

1981   **Break**   Nicollet Island Ampitheatre
        Music: George Lewis   Sponsored by Walker Art
        Sets by local grade school   Center
            children
        performed by 25 people

1981   **IO:** Prologue Performance   Dance Theater Workshop
            for Bicycle, Voice, Slide   New York City
            and Dress
        Text: Bill T. Jones
        Lighting: William Yehle
        Second Section: Set by Bill
            T. Jones

1981   **Ah! Break it!**   Werkcentrum Dans
        Music: Jalalu Calvert Nelson   Rotterdam, Holland
            with additional recorded
            chants by Bill T. Jones
        performed by 12 dancers

1982   **Three Dances**   Harvard University
        Music: Mozart and Peter   Cambridge, Massachusetts
            Gordon
        Text: Bill T. Jones

Shared Distance (1982)
Bill T. Jones and Julie West
photo: Chris Harris

1982   **Shared Distance**   The Kitchen
        Duet with Julie West   New York City

1982   **Long Distance**   The Kitchen
        Solo with artist Keith Haring   New York City

1982   **Duet X 2**   The Kitchen
        Danced first with Rob   New York City
            Besserer, then with Brian
            Arsenault
        Music: Bach air sung by
            Brian Arsenault

1983   **Fever Swamp**   Commissioned by the Alvin
        Music: Peter Gordon   Ailey American Dance
        Sets & Costumes: Bill Katz   Theater
        Lighting: Rick Nelson   First performance: Santa
                                            Monica Civic Auditorium
                                        Santa Monica, California

        Made for television: PBS Great Performances **Three by Three**

Fever Swamp (1988) CUNY
photo: Paula Court

1983	**Naming Things**
	Collaboration with Phillip
	  Mallory Jones and David
	  Hammons
	Music: Miles Davis and
	  traditional funeral dirge
	Performed by 3 Dancers
		Just Above Midtown Gallery
		New York City

1983	**21** Solo performance Recreated for video with Tom Bowes, 1984	Recreation Center Waterloo, Iowa
1983	**Corporate Whimsy** Music: Bryon Rulon Performed by 12 dancers	Tisch School of the Arts New York University New York City
1983	**Casino** Music: Peter Gordon Set: Robert Longo Extended company work using 12 students	Ohio University Athens, Ohio
1984	**Dances with Brahms** Music: Johannes Brahms Two versions: a—Bill T. Jones and 3 women b—solo for Bill T. Jones Costume: Jimmy Myers	Paula Cooper Gallery New York City Leuven, Belgium
1985	**1,2,3** Music: Carl Stone Lighting: Robert Wierzel Set & Costumes: Bill T. Jones	Joyce Theater New York City
1985	**Holzer Duet . . . Truisms** With Lawrence Goldhuber Text: Jenny Holzer Tape Collage: Bill T. Jones	Joyce Theater New York City
1985	**M.A.K.E.** Recorded Text: Bill T. Jones and Arnie Zane Decor: Bill T. Jones	Joyce Theater New York City

Holzer Duet . . . Truisms
(1985) Bill T. Jones and
Lawrence Goldhuber, City
University of New York
photo: Paula Court

**Bill T. Jones and Virgil
Thompson** (1986)
photo: Betty Freeman

Louise Nevelson
photo: Arnie Zane

1985	**Pastiche**
	Visuals: Found Lantern Slides
	   from Arnie Zane
	Music: James Brown, Edith
	   Sitwell, Eric Dolphy
	Text: Bill T. Jones, William
	   Shakespeare
	Lighting: Robert Wierzel
	Crown: Marcel Fieve
		Joyce Theater
		New York City

1986	**Virgil Thompson Etudes**
	Music: Virgil Thompson
	Costume: Louise Nevelson
	   and William Katz
	Lighting: Craig Miller
		Chanterelle
		New York City
		Commissioned for Virgil
		   Thompson's 90th Birthday
		   Celebration

1987	**Red Room**
	Music: Stuart Arbright and
	   Robert Longo
	Set: Robert Longo
		Rockwell Hall
		Buffalo, New York
		(Commissioned for Robert
		   Longo's performance epic
		   Killing Angels)

1988	**Chatter** Music: Paul Lansky	American Dance Festival Durham, North Carolina
1988	**Soon** Music: Kurt Weill, Bessie Smith	Celebrate Brooklyn Festival Prospect Park, Brooklyn, New York

1989	**Don't Lose Your Eye**
	Music: Sonny Boy Williamson
	   and Paul Lansky
		Commissioned for Path
		   Dance Company
		Baltimore, Maryland

1989	**Forsythia** Music: Dufay Recorded Dreamtext: Arnie Zane	Joyce Theater New York City
1989	**La Grande Fête** Music: Paul Lansky Costumes & Masks: Dain Marcus	Joyce Theater New York City

1989	**It Takes Two**
	Music: Ray Charles, Betty
	   Carter
	Lights: Raymond Dooley
		Commissioned by Terry
		   Creach and Stephen
		   Koester
		Dance Theater Workshop
		New York City

1989   **Absence**   Joyce Theater
        Music: Krzysztof Penderecki,   New York City
            Hector Berlioz
        Costumes: Marina Harris
        Lights & Decor: Robert
            Wierzel

1989   **D-Man in the Waters**   Joyce Theater
        Music: Felix Mendelsohn   New York City
        Costumes: Demian   Commissioned in part by St.
            Acquavella and Company   Lukes Chamber Orchestra
        Lighting: Robert Wierzel

Soon (1988)
photo: Maya Wallach

CHOREOGRAPHY: ARNIE ZANE	FIRST PERFORMED
1973 **Self-Portrait** Music: Enrico Caruso Slides: Arnie Zane	Santa Cruz Theatre 103 Santa Cruz, California
1975 **Rhada, a real dance** Collaboration with Peer Bode Performed by 10 dancers	American Dance Asylum Binghamton, New York
1976 **Couple #513** Collaboration with Lois Welk Video: Meryl Blackman	Everson Museum Syracuse, New York
1976 **Transport Dance** Music: Ross Levinson Performed by 14 dancers	American Dance Asylum Binghamton, New York
1976 **At the Crux of** Text and Visuals: Arnie Zane Performed by 10 dancers	American Dance Asylum Binghamton, New York

At the Crux of (1976)
photo: Arnie Zane

1977   **Crux, an Old Dance**   American Dance Asylum
        Constructed Anew   Binghamton, New York
        Performed by 10 dancers

1977   **Steppin'**   American Dance Asylum
        Music: Pierre Ruiz   Binghamton, New York
        Performed by 3 dancers

1977   **Hand Dance**   American Dance Asylum
        Music: Rhys Chatham's   Binghamton, New York
        "Green Line Poem"
        Decor: Arnie Zane
        Duet for Bill T. Jones and
           Arnie Zane

1978   **Hand Dance/Pink Dress Blue** Susquehanna, Pennsylvania
        Music: Helen Thorington
        Decor: Sherry Steiner
        Performed by 7 dancers

1980   **Pieman's Portrait**   Warren Street Performance
        Music: Ross Levinson   Loft
        Performed by 6 dancers   New York City

1981   **Cotillion**   The Kitchen
        Music: Ross Levinson   New York City
        Costumes: Betsey Johnson
        Performed by 9 dancers and
           four musicians

Cotillion (1981) Arnie Zane
and Victoria Marks
photo: Paula Court

1981   **Garden**   Danspace, Saint Mark's
        Collaboration with Johanna   Church
           Boyce   New York City
        Film Clip: **Night and Fog**
        Text: Johanna Boyce
        Music: Traditional Swiss and
           German
        Costumes: Johanna Boyce

1981   **Your Hero**   P.S. 122
        Performed by 5 dancers   New York City
        Text and Music: Bill T. Jones
           and Johanna Boyce

1982   **New Hero**   Riverside Dance Festival
        Performed by 4 dancers   New York City

1982	**Continuous Replay** (solo version of **Hand Dance**) Music: Bryan Rulon	The Kitchen New York City
1983	**Rumble in the Jungle** Music: Max Roach	Riverside Dance Studio London, England
1985	**Peter and the Wolf** Performed by 22 dancers Score: Prokofiev, manipulated by Arnie Zane	SUNY College at Purchase Purchase, New York
1985	**Black Room** Music: Yoshi Wada Duet performance for Bill T. Jones and Heywood McGriff, Jr. Lighting: Robert Wierzel	University of Nebraska Lincoln, Nebraska
1985	**Lotus Eaters** Music: Lorenzo Ferrare Costumes: Michael Jordan Lighting: Robert Wierzel	Joyce Theater New York City

Black Room (1985)
Heywood McGriff, Jr. and
Bill T. Jones

1987   **The Gift/No God Logic**   Saint Mark's Church
        Music: Aria from Verdi's **La**   New York City
            Forza del Destino
        Costumes: Demian
            Acquavella
        Lighting: Robert Wierzel
        Performed by 4 dancers

Lotus Eaters (1985)

1988   **Prejudice** (trio)   Cleveland, Ohio
        Music: Astor Piazzolla
        Lighting: Robert Wierzel
        Costumes: Arnie Zane

1988   **Like in Egypt** (trio)   Cleveland, Ohio
        Music: Traditional Middle
            Eastern
        Lighting; Robert Wierzel
        Costumes: Demian
            Acquavella

Continuous Replay (1983)
photo: Chris Harris

Bill T. Jones/Arnie Zane & Co.

Past Company Members

John Brooks	Karen Pearlman
Poonie Dobson	Amy Pivar
Margaret Liston	Julie West
Heywood "Woody" McGriff, Jr.	Elaine Wright
Jora Nelstein	Vernon Sharpe

Present Company Members (1988)

Demian Acquavella	Bill T. Jones
Arthur Aviles	Heidi Latsky
Sean Curran	Janet Lilly
Lawrence Goldhuber	Bunty Matthais
Gregg Hubbard	Betsy McCracken

Of Heaven and Earth
(1974)
photo: Arnie Zane

Selected Bibliography

Baumsten, Shelley. "Jones/Zane Troupe in 'Secret Pastures,'" *The Los Angeles Times*, January 14, 1985.

Berman, Janice. "In Brooklyn, Time to Dance," *New York Newsday*, July 22, 1988.

Daly, Ann. "BAM and Beyond: The Postmoderns Get Balleticized," *High Performance*, Issue 38, June 1987.

Dunning, Jennifer. "Jones and Zane at The Joyce," *The New York Times*, December 11, 1985.

———. "Bill T. Jones and Arnie Zane at Next Wave," *The New York Times*, December 4, 1986.

———. "Dance: Jones & Zane," *The New York Times*, June 21, 1987.

———. "Bill T. Jones/Arnie Zane & Company," *The New York Times*, May 15, 1988.

Freligh, Becky. "Leaping Over the Barriers," *The (Cleveland) Plain Dealer*, January 10, 1988.

Jowitt, Deborah. "Does My Answer Match Your Question?," *The Village Voice*, March 10, 1980.

———. "Tell Us Your Story," *The Village Voice*, April 28, 1981.

———. "It's Not the Volume, It's the Resonance that Counts," *The Village Voice*, March 15, 1983.

———. "Live From Your Cathode-Ray Tube," *The Village Voice*, December 4, 1984.

———. "Taming the 1980s," *The Village Voice*, December 31, 1985.

———. "Tending the Social Fabric," *The Village Voice*, June 7, 1988.

Kisselgoff, Anna. "Dance: Jones and Zane," *The New York Times* December 13, 1985.

———. "Experimental Works Are Not Necessarily Built to Last," *The New York Times*, December 21, 1986.

Kreemer, Connie. *Further Steps: Fifteen Choreographers On Modern Dance.* New York: Harper & Row, 1987.

Kriegsman, Alan M. "Bill T. Jones' multifarious Movement," *The Washington Post*, February 17, 1982.

———. "Jones, Zane & Company," *The Washington Post*, October 22, 1984.

Laine, Barry. "Trendy Twosome," *Ballet News*, August 1985.

———. "Dance Troupe with Multimedia Flair," *The New York Times*, December 8, 1985.

Lichtman, Cathy. "Collaborative Choreography: Bill T. Jones/Arnie Zane & Co." *City Arts*, Detroit, Michigan, January 1988.

Miodini, Cate. "The Morality of Bill T. Jones and Min Tanaka,"*Dance Pages*, December 21, 1986.

Rosenberg, Donald. "Radical Choreographers Use Medium for Message," *The Beacon Journal* (Cleveland, Ohio), January 8, 1988.

Smith, Amanda. *Dance Magazine*, November 1981.

Supree, Burt. "Any Two Men on the Planet," *The Village Voice*, March 18, 1981.

———. "The Daily Fact of Absence," *The Village Voice*, June 28,1988.

Wallach, Maya. "Bill T. Jones & Arnie Zane: Harmony Born of Contrasts," *The New York City Tribune*, July 22, 1988.

Blauvelt Mountain (1980)
photo: Chris Harris